Inside the Ancient World

AENEAS AND THE ROMAN HERO

INSIDE THE ANCIENT WORLD
General Editor: Michael Gunningham

The following titles are available in this series:

*Denotes books which are especially suited to GCSE or studies at a comparable 16+ level. The remainder may be useful at that level, but can also be used by students on more advanced courses.

Inside the Ancient World

AENEAS AND THE ROMAN HERO

R.D. Williams

BRISTOL CLASSICAL PRESS

General Editor: Michael Gunningham

This impression 2002
This edition published in 1999 by
Bristol Classical Press
an imprint of
Gerald Duckworth & Co. Ltd.
61 Frith Street, London W1D 3JL
Tel: 020 7434 4242
Fax: 020 7434 4420
inquiries@duckworth-publishers.co.uk
www.ducknet.co.uk

Formerly published by Macmillan Education Ltd, 1973
Thomas Nelson and Sons Ltd, 1992

© 1973 by R.D. Williams

A catalogue record for this book is available
from the British Library

ISBN 1 85399 589 4

Contents

List of Illustrations

General Editor's Preface

To get *inside* the Ancient World is no easy task. What is easy is to idealise the Greeks and Romans, or else to endow them unconsciously with our own conventional beliefs and prejudices. The aim of this series is to illuminate selected aspects of Antiquity in such a way as to encourage the reader to form his own judgement, from the inside, on the ways of life, culture and attitudes that characterised the Greco-Roman world. Where suitable, the books draw widely on the writings (freshly translated) of ancient authors in order to convey information and to illustrate contemporary views.

The topics in the series have been chosen both for their intrinsic interest and because of their central importance for the student who wishes to see the civilisations of Greece and Rome in perspective. The close interaction of literature, art, thought and institutions reveals the Ancient World in its totality. The opportunity should thus arise for making comparisons not only within that world, between Athens and Sparta, or Athens and Rome, but also between the world of Antiquity and our own.

The title 'Classical Studies' (or 'Classical Civilisation') is featuring more and more frequently in school timetables and in the prospectuses of universities. In schools, the subject is now taught at Advanced Level as well as at Key Stages 3 and 4. It is particularly for the latter courses that this new series has been designed; also as a helpful ancillary to the study of Latin and Greek in the sixth form and below. (Professor Williams gives the passages he quotes from Virgil both in the original and in translation.) It is hoped that some of the books in the series will interest students of English and History at these levels as well as the non-specialist reader.

The authors, who are teachers in schools or universities, have each taken an aspect of the Ancient World. They have tried not to give a romanticised picture but to portray, as vividly as possible, the Greeks and the Romans as they really were.

The author's object in *Aeneas and the Roman Hero* has been to explain and illustrate the ideals of the newly-founded Roman Empire as they are reflected in Virgil's *Aeneid*. The poem was written at a time when national and patriotic hopes were high, when it seemed that Rome had left behind the sufferings and bloodshed of a series of civil wars, and was poised to enter a period of peace and prosperity, and to spread to the rest of the world the benefits of her civilisation.

In the *Aeneid* Virgil explores the advantages and the problems which this world-destiny involves by symbolising them in an epic narrative – the story of Rome's first founder, the Trojan prince Aeneas. We see in him a person devoted to the high ideals of his mission, ready to sacrifice his personal life for the benefit of future generations: to the best of his ability he follows what he sees as his divine duty. Yet in the course of doing so he is involved in dilemma after dilemma: he must give up his love for Dido (and so destroy her happiness and finally her life itself); he must fight against violent opposition, though he wishes to be a man of peace. He must decide at each and every point how to deal with the human problems which constantly beset him. He must be a new type of hero appropriate for the new Roman world as Virgil saw it – not aggressive or self-seeking, yet brave and firm.

Virgil's portrayal of Aeneas' efforts to achieve this kind of leadership is so sensitively done as to show that the problems of a Trojan prince who lived 3000 years ago shed light on the perpetual problems of the human race. This perhaps is what great poems are about – they illuminate what is universal by their treatment of the particular: and this is why, in Professor Williams's view, Virgil's *Aeneid* continues to be one of the important poems of our civilisation.

January 1973   MICHAEL GUNNINGHAM

Acknowledgements

The publishers wish to acknowledge the following sources of photographs:

Ashmolean Museum pp. 18, 37, 40

Trustees of the British Museum pp. 27, 37

Fototeca Unione & American Academy, Rome pp. 29, 30

Giraudon, Paris p. 10

The Mansell Collection p. 15

The Vatican Museum, Rome p. 45

Illustrations on pages 40 and 71 were taken by the author.

Virgil and the Muses (Mosaic from Sousse)

I

Virgil's life and times

PUBLIUS VERGILIUS MARO (his name in English is generally spelt 'Virgil') was regarded by the Romans as their greatest poet, and most lovers of poetry ever since have agreed. His influence on the Romans themselves, from the time of his younger contemporary Ovid onwards, was profound and his works immediately became school and university text books as well as sources of inspiration for poets, critics, and thinkers; they have remained so for more than two thousand years.

The reasons for admiration have been diverse – always his diction and the music of his hexameter, often his perfection of structure and form, sometimes his ethical and religious message, sometimes the drama of his narrative, sometimes the pathos of the 'tears in things', sometimes his reflection of the Roman character, sometimes his love for the traditions and customs of remote Roman antiquity. All of these things are present in the *Aeneid*, and different generations have admired some more than others according to their own viewpoints; no other poet of the ancient world has had such influence over such a wide area of different literary interests.

Virgil was born in 70 BC near Mantua, in North Italy; his father was a peasant with a small farm, and throughout Virgil's poetry can be seen his love of the Italian land and the simple virtues of the people who cultivated it. He received the best possible education of the time, first at Cremona, then Milan, then Rome. He would have received a thorough training in the Greek and Roman poets, and in rhetorical method and philosophy; his knowledge of Greek and of the Greek way of life was detailed and profound. His whole life was that of a poet and a scholar; he played no part personally in military or political life, and is said to have been somewhat delicate in health and shy and retiring in personality. But as we shall see he took a great interest in Roman national affairs, and was closely in touch with current events through his friendship with men who were directing the movement of affairs, such as Pollio, Gallus, Maecenas, and the Emperor Augustus himself.

His earliest certain work (there are some minor poems ascribed to him, few of which are genuine) was the collection of ten pastoral poems known as the *Eclogues* ('Selections'). These were composed between 42 and 37 BC, and they brought him immediate recognition; he became an important member of the literary court circle under the patronage of Maecenas, to whom he dedicated the *Georgics*, his next work (composed between 37 and 30 BC). This is a treatise in four books about agriculture, designed not so much to provide systematic instruction as to inspire his readers with a love of the land and portray the rewards of the farmer's hard work.

After the publication of the *Georgics* in 30 BC Virgil dedicated himself to the epic poem for which he had been preparing himself all through his life. We know he had thought of and rejected certain themes, such as a poem on the Alban kings or on the exploits of Augustus; the subject he finally chose was the legendary origin of Rome through the foundation in Italy by Aeneas of Lavinium, which founded Alba Longa, which founded Rome. Aeneas was an exile from Troy after it was sacked by the Greeks (in the twelfth century BC) because of the capture of Helen by Paris, and it was laid upon him as a divine mission to take his companions to a western land to found a city which would, as the centuries rolled by, achieve world dominion and civilise all mankind. The choice of the subject satisfied Virgil for many reasons – in the first place the legend, though very well known, was fluid and could be adapted and re-arranged for poetic purposes (for example Dido did not figure at all in the prose version of the legend); secondly it was national and Roman but not too close to history; thirdly it was set in the distant past and could contain elements of adventure and other-worldly imagination like Homer's *Odyssey*; fourthly it could combine past and present over a span of more than a thousand years: its setting is the distant past, but by means of dreams and prophecies, and descriptions of the first celebrations of well-known contemporary customs (foreshadowing Roman values in the character of her first founder Aeneas), it could also be contemporary.

Virgil spent eleven years on the composition of his poem, and in 19 BC, when he planned to spend another three years working on it, he undertook a journey to Greece to get local colour for the revision of the Greek parts of the poem. He fell ill on the journey and returned to Italy but died soon after landing at Brundisium. His dying wish was that the poem should be burnt, but the Emperor Augustus forbade this and the poem was published posthumously.

Essentially the *Aeneid* is a national poem, a picture of Roman character and ideals written at a time when optimism was in the air and the Romans felt that a new and glorious chapter was on the point of opening. Virgil shared in the hope and excitement of the time, and wrote his poem to explore what the Romans were like, what they should be like, and what they could teach the world. To understand the climate of public opinion which the poem reflects (and leads) we should look briefly at the historical circumstances of the time.

Virgil began to compose the *Aeneid* immediately after the inauguration of the Roman Empire following the battle of Actium in 31 BC. At this battle Augustus (Octavian as he was then called) defeated his fellow countryman Antony who was aided by Cleopatra, and the long period of civil war came to an end. The whole of Virgil's life had been lived in a period of impending or actual civil war; when he was born the civil war between Marius and Sulla had not long been ended, and the sparring for position between Julius Caesar and Pompey culminated in 49 BC, when Caesar crossed the Rubicon and a year later defeated Pompey's forces at Pharsalus. Julius Caesar's period of supremacy was short-lived; the daggers of the conspirators struck home on the Ides of March, 44 BC, and there followed what must have been the worst period of all, with constant fighting between rival groups in Italy. The defeat of Brutus and Cassius at Philippi in 42 BC did not end the internal struggle; Sextus Pompeius and his rebels were not finally defeated until 36 BC, and the Roman world then awaited the final showdown between the victors of Philippi, Octavian (Augustus) and Mark Antony. This came eventually at Actium in 31 BC, and Augustus became undisputed master of the Roman world.

Not surprisingly the Romans had felt guilt as well as fear during this long period of civil war: these feelings are well reflected in two of Horace's *Epodes* (written in the last and worst ten years before Actium). Here is a paraphrase of the beginning of *Epode* 16:

> Another generation is now being worn away by civil wars, and Rome rushes to destruction by her own strength. Rome survived Porsena and the Germans and Hannibal, and we ourselves are destroying her, we a wicked generation of guilt-laden stock, and the land on which Rome stands will be possessed again by wild beasts.

Virgil had had personal experience of the miseries of the civil wars when farms around Mantua (perhaps including his own) were confiscated for the resettlement of demobilised soldiers after Philippi, and the first and ninth of his *Eclogues* are about the wretched plight of the dispossessed. In *Eclogue* 1 (64 f.) the shepherd Meliboeus laments that he must leave his farm and go far away, and never again see his little cottage and his corn-crop growing in the fields. 'Shall some accursed soldier possess my beautiful fields, some barbarian my crops? See to what misery civil war has brought us!'

At the end of *Georgics* 1 (written just before Actium) Virgil appeals to the gods to permit Octavian to save the Romans from their sad plight:

> Oh permit this young man to save our ruined generation! Long enough now have we with our blood atoned for the perjury of Laomedon's Troy . . . right and wrong are turned topsy-turvy, there

are wars everywhere in the world, every shape of sin, no proper honour paid to the plough, the fields go to rack and ruin in the absence of the farmers, and the ploughshares are beaten into swords.

And the passage ends with a comparison of the state of affairs in the Roman world with a runaway chariot where the charioteer cannot control the horses.

After Actium Rome got a charioteer who could exercise control in the person of her first Emperor. What wonder that the Roman people, and not least the poets, felt that the long nightmare was over, and that their world had returned at last to sanity? The feeling of relief gave way to one of positive optimism; Rome could now be true to her real self, and achieve what never had been achieved before. These were the hopes prevalent during the first dozen years of Augustus' rule, when the *Aeneid* was being written.

The policy of Augustus, now that he was master of the world (whatever his policies may have been earlier, and there is evidence that he was often ruthless) was aimed essentially at moderation and stability. He had to avoid the mistakes of Julius Caesar, and cloak his absolute authority behind the appearance of constitutional rule and the restoration of the Republic. Apart from the political necessity he seems to have been a genuine lover of the old Roman tradition, and in his social and religious policy as well as in his constitutional settlements he aimed to restore the old way of life, to seek to encourage the qualities which in the past had made Rome great, and could again make her greater still. He sought to bring back the *mos maiorum*, the 'custom of our ancestors', and in this he had the strong support of very many Romans, certainly including Virgil.

But first and foremost Augustus proclaimed that he had brought peace: he twice closed the gates of the temple of Janus which were open in times of war (and had been open through almost all Rome's tempestuous history), and the fighting which took place in his reign was always on the frontiers or in remote parts of the Empire. The citizens of Rome could indeed feel that peace had at last been restored.

We need not here dwell on Augustus' constitutional settlements in which he 'handed back the state to the people', and 'held more prestige but no more power than his colleagues' (these are quotations from his auto-biography, the *Res Gestae*). He avoided in fact all appearance of power-seeking or megalomania. But his social and religious ideas are very relevant to a study of the *Aeneid* because they were shared by Virgil, as indeed by very many of the Romans.

We can read in the preface to Livy's history, written at the beginning of Augustus' reign, a lament for the a.␣␣ent virtues of the Romans and a complaint that the general standard of conduct had greatly declined in his

Statue of Augustus (Prima Porta)

own days. Augustus set out to remedy this, as far as possible, by legislation, and eventually in 18 BC a series of *Leges Iuliae* set limits to expenditure, encouraged family life, penalised sexual laxity. This represented the feeling of many Romans in these years; how far such moral aims can be achieved by legislation is always doubtful (as Horace said: 'What is the use of laws without moral standards to back them?'), but what is plain is that Augustus was expressing the attitude and wishes of many of his subjects

15

when he attempted this legislation (Horace in *Odes* 4.15 praises Augustus for having put bounds to licence, removed sin, and brought back the old way of life by which Rome had grown great).

Similarly in the area of religion Augustus tried to encourage a return to the old standards. He restored the temples that had fallen into disuse (eighty-two of them, according to the *Res Gestae*); he revived ancient cults and ceremonies wherever he could. Here again he was in tune with many contemporaries: in a severe poem (*Odes* 3.6) Horace tells the Romans that they will have to pay for the sins of their ancestors until they restore the temples and crumbling shrines of their ancient gods. Augustus regarded himself as especially under the patronage of Apollo, and built a splendid new temple to Apollo on the Palatine: always and in every way he showed himself the champion of the traditional religion.

What was the relationship of the *Aeneid* to these governmental policies? Quite simply Virgil (like many others) thought along broadly the same lines. No one could have loved the ancient traditions of Rome more than Virgil did, and the qualities by which Rome in the past had grown great – religion, devotion to duty, loyalty, family affection – were those which, by upbringing and personal inclination, he most admired. He was a quite close friend of Augustus, and he must often have discussed with the Emperor the prospects and hopes for a new positive way of life, based upon the old values. The emperor and the poet had the same ideas – not without very good reason. The *Aeneid* reflects the governmental policy of Augustus in moral, social and religious ideas, not because they were Augustus' ideas but because they were Virgil's. When the question is asked, as it often is, 'Did Augustus exert pressure on Virgil to write the *Aeneid*?' (or 'Is the *Aeneid* a piece of governmental propaganda?'), the answer should be that Augustus was just as responsible for the *Aeneid* (and no more so) as Virgil was responsible for the social and religious reforms which Augustus inaugurated. Both men saw things the same way; one acted by political power, the other by poetry.

2
Rome's destiny: The Golden Age

THERE can be no doubt that it was Virgil's primary intention in the *Aeneid* to portray the hopes and aspirations which have been outlined in the previous chapter. The feeling abroad in the first years of Augustus' rule was one of excited optimism – it seemed that after the horrors of civil war Rome had at last found again her true self, and Virgil (like Horace in his Roman Odes, Book 3.1–6) was inspired by this feeling, and set out to portray it in epic form. As the poem took shape, however, it became more apparent to Virgil that the Roman destiny could not in fact be achieved without great sacrifices, suffering and devotion on the part of the Romans themselves, and also disaster to those who stood in the way (like Dido, Turnus, and countless Latin and Rutulian warriors). So powerful was Virgil's sympathy for the defeated that it often seems to conflict with the triumph of Rome's achievement – especially when Dido is brushed aside and trampled upon by its requirements; but the Roman vision is never quite lost sight of, and indeed often is powerfully predominant. The pathos and suffering which it involved will be discussed in another chapter – here we may concentrate first on defining and appreciating the optimistic side of Rome's destiny.

We may best illustrate this from four great patriotic passages in the poem, interlinking them with a brief account of the intervening narrative and of the shorter indications of Roman greatness which occur throughout. The four major passages are: (i) Jupiter's prophecy in Book 1; (ii) the pageant of Roman heroes in Book 6; (iii) the pictures on Aeneas' shield in Book 8; (iv) the reconciliation between Juno, great opponent of Rome, and Jupiter in Book 12.

(i) Jupiter's prophecy (*Aen.* 1.257–96)

The poem begins with a firm statement of how Aeneas was destined by fate (line 2, *fato profugus*) to leave Troy and found a new city in Latīum (i.e. Lavinium) which would be transferred first to Alba Longa and then to Rome. The queen of heaven, Juno, is opposed to this destiny because

B

of her hatred for the Trojans and love of Carthage (fated to be overcome by Rome); she arouses a storm, causing the Trojans to be shipwrecked on the coast of Carthage. Venus, mother of Aeneas and protecting deity of the Roman people, goes to Jupiter and indignantly asks why the promised glory of Aeneas and his Trojan-Roman descendants is· thus being frustrated. Jupiter replies in a serene survey of what Rome is destined to achieve, and promises that it will indeed come to pass. He tells her (1.261 ff.) that Aeneas will wage a great war in Italy, crush their proud peoples, and establish for his nation a way of life and a new city.

Venus Erycina (Coin of Considianus)

Ascanius, his son, also called Iulus, will succeed to his kingdom and found Alba Longa, and three hundred years later Romulus and Remus will be born of the priestess Ilia (Rhea Silvia) and the god Mars; Romulus will found Rome and call the people Roman after his name. 'To these' (promises Jupiter, 1.278 ff.) 'I set no bounds in space or time – I have given them rule without end.' Imagine the impact of this tremendous promise on Virgil's contemporaries – a world empire, unending, under divine providence. Jupiter goes on to promise that Juno will be reconciled (as she is in Book 12) and will join with him in cherishing the Romans, 'rulers of the world, the race wearing the toga' (282). One day Greece will be conquered – we remember how the Greeks have just destroyed Troy, from which Aeneas is a homeless fugitive. There will be born from the stock of Aeneas' son Iulus a Caesar of Julian race (notice how Virgil uses the etymology of Iulus–Julius) who will extend his empire to the Ocean (i.e. the boundaries of Europe) and his fame to the stars. This is Augustus Caesar, adopted son of Julius Caesar, and thus of Julian race. One day, continues Jupiter to Venus, you will receive him in heaven; he too will become a god. And his speech ends with an inspiring promise of peace throughout the world, concord among all people, conquest of violence and hatred. Here it is in Virgil's Latin:

> aspera tum positis mitescent saecula bellis;
> cana Fides et Vesta, Remo cum fratre Quirinus
> iura dabunt; dirae ferro et compagibus artis
> claudentur Belli portae; Furor impius intus
> saeva sedens super arma et centum vinctus aënis
> post tergum nodis fremet horridus ore cruento.

(1.291–6)

And here in Dryden's spirited and vigorous translation (1697):

> Then dire debate and impious war shall cease,
> And the stern age be softened into peace:
> Then banished faith shall once again return,
> And vestal fires in hallowed temples burn.
> And Remus with Quirinus shall sustain
> The righteous laws, and fraud and force restrain.
> Janus himself before his fane shall wait,
> And keep the dreadful issues of his gate,
> With bolts and iron bars; within remains
> Imprisoned Fury, bound in brazen chains;
> High on a trophy raised, of useless arms,
> He sits, and threats the world with vain alarms.

This is indeed a prospect for which men then, as now, might well strive: this is the hope in which the *Aeneid* was conceived. It did not wholly come true – yet the achievement of the Romans, as civilisers and law-givers in the Mediterranean world for more than four centuries after Virgil's times, was such as not to be entirely unworthy of these majestic and splendid prophecies.

(ii) The pageant of Roman heroes (*Aen.* 6.756–853)

The progress of Aeneas towards the fulfilment of his mission through the first six books of the poem will be described in the next chapter; here, however, we may notice a number of passages, especially prophecies and visions which define the nature of Rome's mission, before discussing the great pageant which ends Book 6.

After the landing of the Trojans on the shores of Africa Virgil tells of the kindly reception which they are given by Dido, queen of Carthage, and of how Dido falls in love with Aeneas and asks to hear the story of his wanderings. The second book describes the fall of Troy, the events of the last night of the city once sovereign in all Asia. It is a book of tragedy, brightened only by occasional glimpses of the greatness of Rome, destined to be born from Troy's ashes. When the wooden horse is taken within the walls, the ghost of Hector appears to Aeneas, telling him to flee from Troy, which is doomed, taking with him Troy's gods in order to found a new city, a mighty one, across the seas (2.293–5). Aeneas is slow to obey this vision, feeling himself bound to join in the last resistance with his comrades, and he has to be reminded by Venus of the need to escape with his family (594–600) because of the absolute inevitability of Troy's downfall. In the escape he loses his wife Creusa, and her ghost reiterates Hector's message – he must escape and found a new city by the river Tiber.

In the third book Aeneas describes the long wanderings of seven years' duration while he tried to discover the destined site of his city. The weariness of the seemingly unending journey is relieved with prophecies of greatness to come (far off in the future as it must have seemed to the storm-tossed exiles): at Delos Apollo prophesies that the house of Aeneas will rule the whole world, and his son's sons, and those who come after (3.97–8); in Crete the Penates (the gods of Troy) appear to Aeneas in a vision and promise him that they will raise his descendants to the stars and give empire to his city (158–9): at Buthrotum the seer Helenus gives a long prophecy of the rest of the voyage, ending with the exhortation that Aeneas should press on and make Troy mighty by his deeds (462). These notes of hope brighten the weary quest for what seem to Aeneas to be 'the ever-receding shores of Italy'.

In the fourth book the vision of Rome fades as Aeneas stays on and on with Dido in Carthage, forgetful of his fate. Finally Jupiter intervenes by sending Mercury to remind him of his destiny. Here are Virgil's words:

> non illum nobis genetrix pulcherrima talem
> promisit Graiumque ideo bis vindicat armis;
> sed fore qui gravidam imperiis belloque frementem
> Italiam regeret, genus alto a sanguine Teucri
> proderet, ac totum sub leges mitteret orbem.
>
> (4.227–31)

This is Jackson Knight's translation (Penguin Classics, 1956):

> It was never for this that the most beautiful goddess, his mother, twice rescued him from his Greek foes. This is not the man she led us to think that he would prove to be. No, he was to guide an Italy which is to be a breeding-ground of leadership and clamorous with noise of war, transmit a lineage from proud Teucer's blood, and subject the whole earth to the rule of law.

The passage is of great importance as defining Rome's two-fold mission – first to rule over warlike Italy, and secondly to bring the whole world beneath the sway of laws. First conquest – then civilisation: this, as we shall see, is the message of Anchises' ghost in Book 6.

Aeneas leaves Dido, not of his own free will but under the compulsion of duty (4.361), and after celebrating funeral games for his father Anchises in the fifth book, arrives in Italy and descends to the underworld to learn from Anchises' ghost in Elysium more about the nature of his future destiny. His experiences in the first two-thirds of the sixth book are gloomy and sad, but when he reaches Elysium and is welcomed by his father the mood changes, and Anchises describes to his son at length the multitude of ghosts of the great Roman heroes waiting by the stream of Lethe to be born into the upper world – as they will be if Aeneas can succeed in his mission of founding Rome.

As Anchises describes the ghosts (756–846) they pass in a pageant before the eyes of the reader's imagination: first the kings of Alba Longa (establishing a mood of tradition and antiquity), and then the first king of Rome, Romulus himself, son of Mars, destined to found a city which will bound its empire by earth's limits and its spirit by those of heaven itself, great mother of men, like Cybele, great mother of gods. So far the pageant has been chronological: now the chronology is broken by more than 700 years as Romulus is followed by Augustus, second founder of Rome. All Virgil's art is employed in the description of Rome's first emperor:

> hic vir, hic est, tibi quem promitti saepius audis,
> Augustus Caesar, divi genus, aurea condet
> saecula qui rursus Latio regnata per arva
> Saturno quondam, super et Garamantas et Indos
> proferet imperium; iacet extra sidera tellus,
> extra anni solisque vias, ubi caelifer Atlas
> axem umero torquet stellis ardentibus aptum.

(6.791–7)

This is Copley's version (Bobbs-Merrill, Indianapolis, 1965):

> Here is the man you've heard so often promised:
> Augustus, son of godhead. He'll rebuild
> a golden age in Latium, land where once
> Saturn was king. Past India, past the Moor
> he'll spread his rule to zones beyond the stars,
> beyond the ecliptic, where Atlas carries heaven,
> and bears on his back the spinning, star-tricked wheel.

The description of Augustus continues with a list of the places he will conquer (the Caspian realms, the Maeotian land, the Nile – this last a reference to his victory over Antony and the Egyptian Cleopatra at Actium in 31 BC), and compares him with Hercules and Bacchus. The point of the comparison is threefold – first in the vast tracts of land all three covered in their various activities, second in the civilising influence they brought, and thirdly in that Hercules and Bacchus were in legend mortal men who for their great services to civilisation were deified; the reader is invited to infer that Augustus too deserves, or will deserve, this distinction.

The pageant continues with the kings of Rome; Virgil pauses on Numa, the second king, because he symbolised for the Romans the non-military aspect of their mission. Romulus, the first king, was a figure of bravery and military strength; Numa is the embodiment of religion and civilisation. Virgil speaks of him as 'conspicuous with his olive branch, carrying the sacred emblems' and as the man who 'will found the little city securely on the basis of law'. The idea of the Romans first as world-conquerors by divine providence, and then as world-civilisers is vividly symbolised in the description of the second king.

After the kings come various heroes of the republic: first Brutus, the founder of the republic, who expelled Tarquin the Proud; then the Decii, the Drusi, Torquatus, Camillus, who saved Rome from the Gauls; then Caesar and Pompey, presented in sad tones because of the civil war which they fought against each other – now, in Augustus' time, hopefully a thing of the past; then the conquerors of Greece and of Carthage, and finally Fabius Maximus, who 'by delaying saved the Roman state'. This is a reference to the most critical period of Roman history, when after his victories at Lake Trasimene and Cannae in 217–16 BC the Carthaginian leader Hannibal appeared to have Rome at his mercy. Fabius, however, by refusing pitched battle and harrying Hannibal wherever he went enabled the Romans to recover their strength and finally prevail. Fabius comes last in the pageant because he symbolises survival, because he exorcises Dido's curse in 4.625 ff. (where she had called for an unknown avenger to arise from her bones), and because he was described by Ennius in a famous line which Virgil quotes, thus adding to the long list of heroes of history a tribute to his great predecessor in literature.

When the pageant is over Anchises summarises the mission of Rome in these lines:

excudent alii spirantia mollius aera
(credo equidem), vivos ducent de marmore vultus,
orabunt causas melius, caelique meatus
describent radio et surgentia sidera dicent:
tu regere imperio populos, Romane, memento
(hae tibi erunt artes), pacique imponere morem,
parcere subiectis et debellare superbos.

(6.847–53)

Others will beat out the breathing bronze in softer lines (I believe it myself), they will bring forth living faces from the marble, they will plead cases better, and describe the wanderings of the heavens with their measuring-rods, and tell of the rising stars. But, Romans, you must remember to rule the peoples with your government (such shall be your arts), and to add civilisation to peace, to spare the conquered and cast down the proud.

It is clear that the first four lines refer to the Greeks. Virgil concedes to them supremacy in sculpture, oratory and astronomy (in all of which the Romans achieved no mean success) in order to emphasise the more strongly the aspects of Roman supremacy. The Roman 'arts' to balance the Greek achievement are in the province of government (*regere imperio*), and government is defined as first achieving peace and then superimposing civilisation (*morem*): finally peace is a matter of sparing the conquered and overthrowing the aggressor. These sonorous lines convey an optimistic picture of Rome's destiny – one which they did not perhaps wholly achieve in the four centuries of Roman imperial power after Augustus, but in which their advances towards a conception of world peace, wise administration, humane tolerance, have left a deep influence upon modern man in the western world. This is in essence what Virgil in the *Aeneid* felt that the Romans could achieve – and they went in fact a long way towards it.

(iii) The shield of Aeneas (*Aen.* 8.626–731)

After the vision of the Roman heroes in the underworld Aeneas returns to his men at Cumae, and they sail north to the Tiber; their arrival at the famous and historic river is described in a passage of idyllic and serene beauty (7.25–36). They are hospitably received by King Latinus, who recognises in their arrival the fulfilment of an oracle that his daughter was to marry a foreigner and from the union of the peoples would arise a race that would raise the Latin name to the stars (7.98–101 and 270–2). But this happy situation is changed by the intervention of Juno, who persuades Turnus the Rutulian, already betrothed to Latinus' daughter Lavinia, to take up arms against the newcomers. War breaks out, and Virgil gives a catalogue of the Italian forces opposing the Trojans, a vivid portrayal of the peoples and places of his beloved Italy. The *Aeneid* presents the paradox of how the defeated (the Italians) in fact contributed much more to the future Roman people than the victorious Trojans (this is discussed more fully in the next section).

Aeneas leaves to get help from Evander, an Arcadian king whose city Pallanteum is built on the site of the seven hills where centuries later Rome was to arise. In the description of Aeneas' visit to the site of Rome which occupies Book 8 Virgil gives a peaceful picture shot through with future destiny. Aeneas visits the famous places of Rome: the Carmental gate, the Lupercal, Argiletum, the Capitol – 'golden now,' says Virgil, 'but then rough ground of thickets and brambles' (8.348). Evander's son Pallas is sent with a contingent of warriors to help Aeneas, and Venus arranges with Vulcan for a new shield to be made for Aeneas.

The idea of describing pictures on a shield is taken from Homer, where Achilles, because Patroclus had borrowed his armour and Hector had despoiled him of it, is provided with a new shield by his goddess mother; the pictures on it are described at length. Aeneas in Virgil has not lost his shield, but what Virgil achieves by giving him a new one is the opportunity of another review of Roman history and achievement comparable with the pageant in Book 6. And he gives it at this very last moment before the full-scale fighting begins in Book 9 so that the reader may once again be reminded of how much depends on the success of Aeneas' mission.

The scenes from Roman history which are depicted on the shield are chosen partly because they lend themselves to pictorial description, and partly as examples of the qualities which the Romans most admired in the heroes of their race, qualities which they hoped they could show again in the future in the revival and expansion of their greatness under Augustus. The first picture shows the twins Romulus and Remus being suckled by the she-wolf: this was the most famous Roman emblem of all, frequently depicted in visual art, especially on coins, and it symbolises the simple origins and powers of survival of the Roman people. There follows a picture of the rape of the Sabine women and the subsequent reconciliation between the Romans and the Sabines, as a result of which the Sabine king, Numa Pompilius, eventually succeeded Romulus – here again is the note of religion and civilisation which Numa symbolised in the pageant. Next is Mettus, suffering a horrible punishment for breaking his promise – the Romans always thought of themselves as people who kept their word, and regarded their enemies, such as the Carthaginians, as perfidious. Next is depicted the attempt by Lars Porsena of Clusium to restore the exiled Tarquin, who had been the last king in Rome; included is a description of Horatius Cocles holding the bridge, and the maiden Cloelia swimming the Tiber.

At the top of the shield there is a picture of how the sacred geese gave the alarm as the Gauls attacked the Capitol; religious ceremonies are depicted in the same scene, and the powerful impression given that the gods had saved Rome from extinction because the Romans were a religious people, chosen for world empire because of their right relationship with the gods. At about the same time as Virgil was composing the *Aeneid* Horace wrote an Ode (*Odes* 3.6) in which he urged the Romans to return to their traditional worship, summarising (line 5) the Roman destiny in the words *dis te minorem quod geris imperas*: 'because you are servants of the gods, you are masters on earth.'

All the pictures described so far have been round the edge of the shield: in the centre are pictures of the battle of Actium, the last battle of Rome's civil war at which in 31 BC Augustus defeated the forces of

Antony and Cleopatra. We see Augustus going into battle, leading the Italians, along with the senate and the people and the gods of Rome (678–9); opposing him with barbarian forces from the East are Antony and Cleopatra, the latter with snakes behind her head (symbolising her suicide through an asp's bite after the battle). The gods of Rome (Neptune, Venus, Minerva, Apollo) are drawn up in battle against the eerie and gruesome deities of the Egyptians, such as the dog-headed Anubis. Next Cleopatra is shown in flight, seeking safety between the banks of the Nile; and finally we see Augustus celebrating his triumph in Rome, with appropriate sacrifices to the gods who have given Rome the victory, and reviewing the conquered peoples who come from the farthest confines of the known earth.

Here is the passage in Virgil:

at Caesar, triplici invectus Romana triumpho
moenia, dis Italis votum immortale sacrabat,
maxima ter centum totam delubra per urbem.
laetitia ludisque viae plausuque fremebant;
omnibus in templis matrum chorus, omnibus arae;
ante aras terram caesi stravere iuvenci.
ipse sedens niveo candentis limine Phoebi
dona recognoscit populorum aptatque superbis
postibus; incedunt victae longo ordine gentes,
quam variae linguis, habitu tam vestis et armis.

(8.714–23)

and this is Dryden's translation:

The victor to the gods his thanks expressed,
And Rome, triumphant, with his presence blessed.
Three hundred temples in the town he placed,
With spoils and altars every temple graced.
Three shining nights and three succeeding days
The fields resound with shouts, the streets with praise,
The domes with songs, the theatres with plays.
All altars flame: before each altar lies,
Drenched in his gore, the destined sacrifice.
Great Caesar sits sublime upon his throne,
Before Apollo's porch of Parian stone:
Accepts the presents vowed for victory,
And hangs the monumental crowns on high.
Vast crowds of vanquished nations march along,
Various in arms, in habit, and in tongue.

These are the pictures on the shield: Aeneas marvels at them (729–31) not knowing what they are, and 'raises on to his shoulder the fame and destiny of his descendants.' In picking up the shield he literally shoulders Rome's history; throughout the poem he metaphorically shoulders the task of inaugurating that history.

(iv) The reconciliation of Jupiter and Juno (*Aen.* 12.791–842)

In order to fulfil the destiny laid upon them the Trojans are forced to fight the opposing forces under Turnus, and the battle scenes of the last four books are fierce and costly to both sides. Venus intervenes again (10.18 ff.) to appeal for her Trojans, and Juno opposes her pleas; the battles continue until finally single combat between Aeneas and Turnus is arranged. Aeneas swears an oath to abide by the result of the single combat (12.176 ff.) in which he promises in the event of victory not to make the Italians subservient to the Trojans, but to join the two peoples under equal conditions. But the Rutulians break the truce, and Juno continues to intervene to help Turnus (as Venus does to help Aeneas) until Jupiter tells Juno that she must now give in. He says that she knows Aeneas is destined for glory, and that her opposition must cease.

Juno yields, asking for one condition. This is that (823 ff.) the Latins shall not have to alter their name and be called Trojans, or change their language or their way of dress. She asks that the Roman stock shall be strong through Italian valour, and that Troy shall vanish. Jupiter accepts her condition.

> do quod vis, et me victusque volensque remitto.
> sermonem Ausonii patrium moresque tenebunt,
> utque est nomen erit; commixti corpore tantum
> subsident Teucri. morem ritusque sacrorum
> adiciam faciamque omnis uno ore Latinos.
> hinc genus Ausonio mixtum quod sanguine surget,
> supra homines, supra ire deos pietate videbis,
> nec gens ulla tuos aeque celebrabit honores.
>
> (12.833–40)

Here is Day Lewis's translation (Hogarth Press and Oxford Paperbacks, 1952):

> Willingly I grant what you ask: you have won me over.
> The Italians shall keep their native tongue and their old traditions;
> Their name shall not be altered. The Trojans will but sink down in
> The mass and be made one with them. I'll add the rites and usage
> Of Trojan worship to theirs. All will be Latins, speaking
> One tongue. From this blend of Italian and Trojan blood shall
> > arise

A people surpassing all men, nay even the gods, in godliness.
No other nation on earth will pay such reverence to Juno.

Temple of Jupiter,
Juno and Minerva on
the Capitol (Coin of
Vespasian)

We notice in these final decrees of Jupiter not merely the acceptance of Italian rather than Trojan supremacy in the mixture of their races which will produce the Roman people, but also the great insistence on the religious qualities of this people that will rule the world. The Roman mission is first to conquer the proud (because the gods wish it so, for the benefit of the human race), and then to establish for all peoples a civilised way of life based on religious worship of the powers greater than themselves.

After this reconciliation in heaven the poem ends quickly on the human plane, as Aeneas wounds and then kills Turnus. The proud have been conquered, Turnus by Aeneas in Virgil's poem, and Antony by Augustus in the real history of Virgil's time – a thousand years later. The road is open for what Pliny called 'the boundless majesty of the Roman peace' (*immensa Romanae pacis maiestas*).

3

Aeneas – the new hero

IN order to present the destiny of Rome as outlined in the previous chapter, Virgil had to create in his hero a prototype of the Roman character, a person who showed by his behaviour the kind of qualities which had made Rome great and would make her greater still. He had to be an ideal Roman with qualities of leadership, a sort of model for Augustus and his successors. (It is a great mistake to think that Aeneas was modelled on Augustus; it is rather the case that Virgil is trying to depict a character upon whom Romans of his day could model themselves.)

In drawing the character of his hero Virgil had chosen a legend which gave him a fairly free hand. Aeneas in Homer is an important Trojan prince, but one whose character is fairly vague: he is brave and religious, but he has no special traits which would have to be reproduced by Virgil (as for example Odysseus or Achilles had). The details of the Aeneas legend in Greek and Latin literature had been very varied, and Virgil could adapt and recast it for his own purposes. To a large extent he could create the character of his hero exactly as he wanted it.

But how did he want it? The very word hero was associated with the heroic age, the days of Mycenae and Troy of which Homer had written, and the qualities of a hero of those times were entirely different from those needed in Virgil's day, when the complex organisation of Rome called for abilities and characteristics of another sort altogether. This was Virgil's problem – to present a character appropriate to be called a hero in a time which (like our own) was no longer 'heroic'. In one sense of course Aeneas does live in the heroic world – he is a contemporary of Achilles and Odysseus, and his dramatic date is twelfth century BC. But in another sense he is the first Roman – he has to foreshadow the qualities of a different civilisation altogether. He has to step out of one world (the world of Troy, finally destroyed by Greek fire) into another, into a western land which will ultimately rule the world. What will be the qualities appropriate for this new civilisation? Obviously not the same as those of the old – but how far different and in what ways?

The character and the ideals of Homer's heroes are fairly easy to define.

Aeneas offering sacrifices (Ara Pacis)

Achilles lived in a world of a simple sort, and knew precisely what was expected of him. He does not have deep intellectual or emotional problems; his is a direct straightforward way of life, in which the honour of the individual is the main and basic standard of behaviour. He has to be true to himself and his reputation, and so act that he preserves his honour and does not fall below what is required of him. He must be brave, and never drop short of the expected standard of bravery which his position as the greatest Greek warrior calls for. His behaviour is always direct, impetuous, spontaneous, not concerned with others except in so far as his behaviour towards them modifies his own individual glory and prowess. Such a figure in Roman society would be hopelessly out of place, and Aeneas had to be drawn differently.

Again, let us make a comparison with Homer's Odysseus. Odysseus, man of many resources, had the task of surmounting endless difficulties in order to return home to his native land of Ithaca where his wife Penelope was loyally awaiting him, in order to resume the old life he had left. Aeneas on the other hand had no home to return to – his home in Troy had been destroyed and he had to find a new home and indeed a new way of life in a far distant country. Odysseus by his superior skill and endurance finally reached home when all his companions, lesser men, had fallen by the wayside; but Aeneas had to reach his new promised land with all his companions safe – otherwise the new settlement could never be founded. In brief the Homeric heroes are great individualists, but

Ara Pacis (South-east corner)

Aeneas has to be the social man, the man who through his care for others succeeds in leading his group or his society, not aiming to achieve personal satisfaction by surpassing others in excellence, but to use his qualities in order to achieve *their* success.

This basic feeling of social responsibility in Aeneas is especially defined by Virgil in the standing epithet he gives to his hero – *pius*. The Latin word is difficult to define briefly in English – essentially it means 'aware of one's responsibility', 'dutiful', 'devoted to others'. It means that such a person puts other considerations before his own interests. This quality of being *pius* (*pietas* is the noun) may be shown by subordinating one's own desire to various other loyalties: (i) to the gods and their requirements, hence our English derivative 'piety'; (ii) to one's country – here the idea of patriotism comes in; (iii) to one's family, a form of devotion to others which the Romans specially esteemed; (iv) to one's friends; and (v) to one's subordinates. Often these different categories may overlap, and it is not always essential to define which one of them is specially relevant at any one time as long as we recognise that this is the essence of the man – he tries to shoulder his responsibilities, to face his obligations. He must not yield to personal ambition or the desire for self-aggrandisement; he must be first and foremost a valuable member of society, commanding respect because it is known that he is not self-seeking.

Now such a person in literature does not always satisfy the desires we may have for the grandiose, the sublime, the superhuman. Aeneas does not cut the figure of an Achilles – he does not stride magnificently through life brushing off all opposition in superior self-confidence of his own ability; and for this failing he has often been censured by the critics. But it is not that Virgil has tried to create another Achilles and failed to do so; it is that he has tried to create an entirely different kind of hero. We may all decide personally whether he has been successful in his new creation – and may well decide that he has not; but we must not judge Aeneas adversely because we think he ought to be like Achilles.

It is time now to look at the way in which Virgil has presented Aeneas in his poem, asking ourselves not 'Has Virgil succeeded in making Aeneas like Achilles?' but 'Has Virgil succeeded in making Aeneas unlike Achilles?' There are three particular aspects of Aeneas' character which can focus our thoughts as we follow him through the poem: (i) has he a free will of his own, or is he too often a puppet? In other words, what is the relationship of a man of destiny to the powers to which he has devoted himself; is there freedom in service to an ideal? (ii) What are the limits of his human strength – is he weak when he should be strong? (iii) Does he always live up to the ideals (which Dryden admired in him) of 'piety to the gods, care of his people, justice in general towards mankind'? We shall find that Virgil has provided a series of situations in which all these problems can be sympathetically examined, in which there is no exaggerated simplification, no suggestion that because Aeneas is strong and good he can easily do what is to be done, but rather an investigation of what is meant by 'strong' and 'good' and how one particular person tried to solve the ever-recurrent problems which fortune sends upon the best of us as well as the worst of us. Above all it is the human experience and problems of Aeneas as a human person (not a super-human person) which are emphasised in the *Aeneid*.

Book 1

Before the narrative begins Virgil tells us in his introduction and invocation the nature of Aeneas' mission, and of his divine calling. In the second line of the poem we learn that Aeneas came to Italy from Troy because he was 'an exile by fate' (*fato profugus*). Fate is all the time behind the human action. This is a main way in which Virgil's poem differs from Homer: in Homer fate indeed governs men's actions, but it is a short-term fate, something which determines the problems of the moment, or at the most of a man's lifetime – but in Virgil fate has its plan for hundreds and thousands of years ahead. In a paradoxical way it requires the co-operation of man for its fulfilment, and this co-operation Aeneas for his part is resolved to give to the utmost of his human ability.

Next we learn of the hostility to Aeneas of Juno. This is explained on several levels – on the mythological level it is because Juno was angry with the Trojans on account of the judgement of Paris, when she was passed over in favour of Aphrodite in a contest of beauty; on the historical level it is because she favours the city of Carthage, the great rival of Rome for Mediterranean supremacy; on the symbolic level she personifies the 'slings and arrows of outrageous fortune', the apparently senseless mis-haps and disasters which come upon men as they strive for worthy ends. Throughout the poem, as we shall see, she opposes Aeneas although she knows she is inferior in power to Jupiter who supports him; and though she cannot ultimately change the fates, she can and does cause such suffering and setbacks as to make it constantly uncertain when and how the fated destiny can come true.

Virgil asks (lines 8–11) what is the cause of this suffering inflicted on the good: 'tantaene animis caelestibus irae?' ('can there be such great anger in heavenly hearts?'). To define the 'good' he uses the noun especially used of Aeneas – *pietas*: if a man shows this quality of self-sacrifice, why must he suffer? The question runs through the poem, and it is not satisfactorily answered; but it is in the exploration of this question and its implications that much of the deepest insight and human sympathy of the *Aeneid* is shown.

The narrative of Book 1 begins when the Trojans, after seven years of wandering, are just leaving Sicily for Italy, on the very last stage of their journey. Juno intervenes and causes a storm, and our first meeting with the hero of the poem is in the midst of this storm. We might expect him to show courage and resolution in the face of this dangerous situation – but in fact he acts otherwise: he is terrified.

> extemplo Aeneae solvuntur frigore membra;
> ingemit et duplicis tendens ad sidera palmas
> talia voce refert: 'o terque quaterque beati,
> quis ante ora patrum Troiae sub moenibus altis
> contigit oppetere! o Danaum fortissime gentis
> Tydide! mene Iliacis occumbere campis
> non potuisse tuaque animam hanc effundere dextra.

(1.92–8)

Straightaway Aeneas' limbs were loosened by cold fear; he groaned and holding out his two hands to the stars thus he spoke: 'O three times and four times fortunate those whose lot it was to fall in death before their parents' eyes beneath the lofty walls of Troy! O son of Tydeus, bravest of the race of the Greeks – could I not have fallen on the plains of Ilium and breathed forth my life, killed by your hand. . . .'

Virgil has most deliberately shown us Aeneas on his first appearance as a frail mortal, put under pressures which are almost too great for him to bear, and under this latest disaster of his seven year wanderings almost ready to give up, and wishing that he were dead. We realise at the outset that the hero of the poem is not someone of superhuman strength who can retain his confidence in all adversity, but rather a brave man near the end of his tether. We wonder here, as we often shall again, whether Aeneas will manage to keep going.

Finally the storm is calmed by Neptune, and in the first simile of the poem Neptune in calming the storm is compared with a statesman calming a violent mob, rioting and hurling stones and torches. Two things are very striking about this simile: first that it is presented as it were the wrong way round, with the world of nature compared with the human world instead of vice versa. Thus it compels our attention for its other aspect: this is that it uses the key words of the poem – *furor* for the violent quality of the mob, and *pietas* for the responsible attitude of the statesman. The task of Aeneas throughout the poem is to try to calm the force of *furor* ('violence', 'madness', 'frenzy') in others and in himself by means of *pietas* ('thought for others'). He does not find it as easy to calm the storms of the human heart as Neptune found it to calm the waves.

Aeneas with some of his ships lands safely in Africa (the remainder, except one, is also safe in another part) and he goes out to forage and organise food and shelter for his men. As the Trojans prepare to restore their strength by feeding on the stags Aeneas has shot, their leader makes a heartening speech:

> o socii (neque enim ignari sumus ante malorum),
> o passi graviora, dabit deus his quoque finem.
> vos et Scyllaeam rabiem penitusque sonantis
> accestis scopulos, vos et Cyclopia saxa
> experti: revocate animos maestumque timorem
> mittite; forsan et haec olim meminisse iuvabit.

(1.198–203)

Friends, we have experienced suffering before, we had suffered worse than this, and the gods will bring this too to an end. You have endured the fury of Scylla and approached those deep-roaring cliffs, you have known the rocks of the Cyclops: rally your courage and

banish sad fear; perhaps one day the memory of this too will be a
cause of joy. . . .

A heartening speech – but Virgil immediately tells us that Aeneas'
confidence was pretended – he was putting a bold face on it: 'Thus he
spoke, and sick at heart with great anxiety he pretended hope in his
expression and hid his anguish deep in his heart' (1.208–9).

Thus in the opening scene Virgil has especially shown us that Aeneas
is a mortal man of limited strength, and has come near to the end of it.
Now the narrative switches to heaven, where Venus complains to Jupiter
of the sufferings her son is undergoing, ending with the phrase *hic pietatis
honos*? – 'Is this the reward for duty well done?' The reader echoes the
feeling of indignation against whatever powers there be. Jupiter's reply
tells in serene and majestic phrases of the glory that awaits Aeneas. This
passage has already been discussed (pp. 18f.) and all that need be added
here is to emphasise the closing image of the speech, the picture of *Furor
impius* in chains, conquered by peace and justice. Here then is the hope that
Aeneas by founding the city destined to become Rome will begin a
process of taming the wickedness and frenzy in human hearts by means of
pietas, devotion to others.

Aeneas sets out to explore the land where he and his men have been
shipwrecked, and he meets his mother, the goddess Venus, disguised as a
huntress. She tells him that he has come to Carthage, where Dido is
queen, and asks who he and his men are. In reply he says that they are
Trojans and that he is Aeneas, man of destiny ('sum pius Aeneas'). This
key word *pius* has already been used of him twice in the narrative (220,
305), and now his own use of it emphasises his knowledge that he is a
man with a calling, a man whose actions must be determined not primarily
by his own wishes and desires but by the requirements of the mission to
which he has dedicated himself. In addition to this his use of the word
here has about it an implied indignation, just like Venus' question to
Jupiter ('is this the reward for duty well done?'). I am trying, says Aeneas,
to fulfil a mission which has been placed upon me, and yet nothing will
go right for me. Here I am, shipwrecked on the coast of Africa, after
having been driven out of Asia and Europe. We see here a man who has
willingly given himself to the fulfilment of a mission, but has by no means
yet acquired the strength and the certainty which will enable him to press
on against all setbacks and over all obstacles. He is frail and human; his
resolution has its limits, and he has nearly reached them. The task he has
undertaken, that of setting going the Roman way of life in a hostile and
alien world, is almost too great for his strength. But he does not give up –
this is the essence of the new kind of heroism.

As Venus leaves him he recognises his goddess mother and rebukes her

– not without reason – for her cruelty to him. 'Why do you so often mock your son with false disguises? You too are cruel' (407–8). He is a solitary and lonely figure, beset by cruel difficulties of all sorts, with his father dead, his son still young, no strong companions to help him. His seconds-in-command are shadowy figures, none more so than his faithful companion Achates, who plays an altogether passive and colourless role in the poem. What a contrast with the Greek heroes in Homer's *Iliad*, strong men supporting each other even without their strongest of all, Achilles: Agamemnon, Menelaus, Odysseus, Diomedes, Ajax, Idomeneus, and countless more. Aeneas has no such powerful support in his mission.

As Aeneas goes with Achates to the city of Carthage he marvels at the activity and achievement of Dido's people, and he gazes on a city rising up out of nothing – his own city, he reflects, is not yet founded: 'O fortunati quorum iam moenia surgunt' (437) – 'Lucky those people whose city walls are already rising.' He looks at the pictures on Juno's temple wall, scenes depicting the war against the Greeks in which he had just fought and lost, and he speaks what are perhaps the most famous phrases of the poem: 'sunt hic etiam sua praemia laudi, sunt lacrimae rerum et mentem mortalia tangunt' (461–2) – 'here too glorious deeds have their reward, here too there are tears for the things that happen, and mortal suffering touches the heart.' Aeneas gains confidence from the knowledge that the Carthaginians too are people who are sympathetic towards suffering and appreciative of bravery, and this confidence is wholly justified in the reception which the Trojans get from Dido, Queen of Carthage. She welcomes them with a serene grace and dignity which is immensely impressive, and Aeneas responds with words of deep gratitude. Gifts are exchanged, a royal banquet prepared – but beneath the idyllic appearance lurk the seeds of tragedy and doom. Through the intervention of Cupid and Venus Dido is made to fall in love with Aeneas, and Virgil insets into his narrative phrases which look forward to the inevitably unhappy outcome – for Aeneas is not free to stay with Dido; he must sacrifice himself and her for the demands of his mission.

Books 2 and 3

At the end of Book 1 Dido asks Aeneas to tell his story, and he does so in the next two books. They are therefore a flashback, earlier in time than the narrative of Book 1, and so they give us our earliest glimpse of the character of Aeneas, and are specially significant because his character emerges from his own words – it is his own version of himself which we read. The second Book tells dramatically and tragically the events of just one night, the night of Troy's downfall; the third Book tells the long and weary story of seven years' wandering and searching for the place of the destined city.

The first part of Book 2 describes how the Trojans were persuaded by Sinon to take the wooden horse filled with Greek warriors into the city. Aeneas himself does not enter the story till after this, when he tells of how, on that night, the ghost of Hector appeared to him in his sleep and told him that Troy was doomed, could no longer be saved – 'if it could have been, it would have been saved by my right hand' (291–2) – and that Aeneas must escape, taking with him the gods of Troy, and found a new city far off over the sea. This is the first indication which Aeneas has had that he is a man with a mission; and his reaction is by no means one of immediate acceptance. Finding the Greeks within the walls he rushes madly out to sell his life dearly:

> arma amens capio; nec sat rationis in armis,
> sed glomerare manum bello et concurrere in arcem
> cum sociis ardent animi; furor iraque mentem
> praecipitat, pulchrumque mori succurrit in armis.

> (2.314–17)

Madly I seized my weapons; nor did I think about it once I had done so but my heart was aflame to gather a force for fighting and rush to the citadel with my companions; frenzy and anger drove on my thoughts, and I decided that death in battle would be a glorious end.

Here we see the Homeric warrior of the heroic age, impetuous, courageous, ready to sell his life dearly, ready with the splendid gesture, the heroic impulse; Aeneas has not yet begun to learn that his mission must preclude the glorious death. His life is not his own to give away; it is owed to those who depend on him. Not for him the grand gesture – he must learn the long hard way of ever struggling on towards his dimly seen goal. He must step out of Homer's world and become the first Roman.

But he is slow to realise this; Hector's message is ignored as he fights madly to try to save those of his friends he can, and to rally them to the defence of the doomed city. 'Let us die,' he cries (353), 'hurling ourselves into the midst of the fighting.' He and his followers are compared with wolves in their frenzy for slaughter (355 ff.); he continues to fight wildly, to try to sell his life dearly; he calls on the ashes of Troy to testify that he did not try to avoid the heat of the battle, and that he had sought death (431 ff.). He feels the heroic warrior's guilt at having escaped when so many brave men died; he cannot yet accept that he must willingly shoulder a different task.

Next he is forced to witness the horrible sight of the death of Priam's son, Polites, and then of the old king himself at the hands of the violent Pyrrhus. Only now for the first time does he think of any of his obligations other than that as a warrior of Troy; now he recalls his own old father, Anchises, perhaps exposed to the same fate as Priam, and his wife Creusa and his little son, Iulus. On his way to his home he meets Helen, the cause of the war, sheltering from the fighting at the temple of Vesta; anger and rage overcome him (575) and he is on the point of killing her when Venus intervenes and stops him. This passage is not in the major manuscripts of Virgil, and though he certainly wrote it there is reason to believe that he may have intended to change it; but what is important is that Virgil's concept of the character of Aeneas while he was still in Troy is such that he could have thought of killing a woman. He is still impetuous, violent, a victim of that angry passion (*furor*) which throughout the poem he attempts – with very incomplete success – to conquer.

The goddess Pietas (obverse) and Aeneas carrying Anchises (reverse) (Coin of Herennius)

Venus urges him to think of his family's safety and to concentrate his thoughts on escape, not vengeance; she shows him the supernatural vision of hostile deities destroying Troy, and convinces him (as Hector had not been able to) that armed resistance is useless. Aeneas cannot at first persuade Anchises to leave, but a supernatural omen convinces him that the gods wish it; and carrying his father on his shoulders, leading his little son by the hand, and with Creusa his wife following behind he sets out to escape. In the confusion Creusa is lost; Aeneas rushes back to find her, but is confronted by her ghost, telling him that she is not destined to

Octavian (obverse) and Aeneas carrying Anchises (reverse) (Coin of Octavian)

come with him. He must travel far over the seas (780 ff.) and find a western land where the river Tiber flows though the fertile fields. All this, she insists, is destined by fate (777–8).

Aeneas now gathers his followers together, and as the dawn rises leads them off into the hills to prepare for their escape over the seas. The long night of Troy's agony is over, and the new dawn portends the new city that will arise from Troy's ashes, the golden city of Rome.

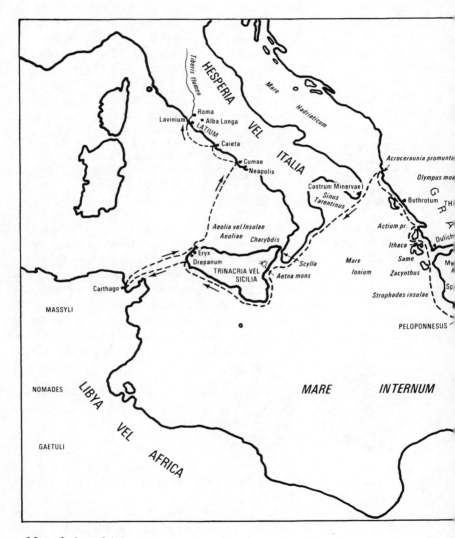

Map of Aeneas' journey

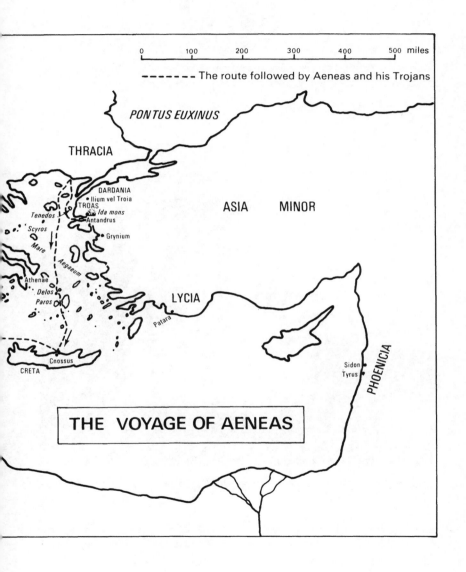

THE VOYAGE OF AENEAS

In the second book then we have seen how Aeneas to begin with was no different from any Homeric hero. He was brave, reckless, inclined to

Aeneas, Anchises and the Palladium (Coin of Caesar)

the heroic gesture. He has to learn a new way of life, and in the long years of the voyage, described in the third book, we see him beginning to learn.

Temple of Vesta in the Roman Forum—traditional home of the sacred objects brought by Aeneas from Troy

As Aeneas had had to endure the sorrow of the loss of his wife and many of his friends in Book 2, so now he must endure the dangers and tedium of the search for his city. It is a story of many false trails, and of oracular assistance given chiefly by Apollo which gradually brings the

Trojans nearer and nearer to their western land. First they land in Thrace where a terrifying omen drives them away; they come to the island of Delos where Apollo tells them to seek out their ancient mother. Mistakenly they think this is Crete, but are turned from that island by a plague. Then the Penates appear to Aeneas telling him that Italy is the aim of their quest. They pass the island of the Harpies and the site of Actium and at Buthrotum receive a long prophecy from Helenus. They land in Italy, but on the wrong side; from here they go to Sicily and round the island, and from there – Aeneas tells Dido – the storm drove him off his course to Italy and on to the coast of Carthage.

Throughout this third book Aeneas learns more about the intentions of the gods for the exiled Trojans, and of how success depends on endurance and especially on a right relation with the gods. Prayers and sacrifices form a recurrent theme in the book, and in this as in all else Aeneas is very greatly helped and encouraged by the guidance of his father Anchises. Anchises gives to Aeneas the encouragement and advice which Aeneas learns it is his duty to give to his son Iulus and to all those dependent on him. At the very end of the voyage, at Drepanum in Sicily, Anchises dies and Aeneas is left to complete his mission on his own.

Book 4

This is the book in which Aeneas comes nearest to abandoning his mission; here, as our attention is concentrated on the pathos of Dido's love for Aeneas, we are furthest of all from thoughts of Rome and Roman destiny. Dido has fallen in love with Aeneas, and he, forgetful for a time of his mission, as he well might be after all he has been through, stays with her during the winter months, not thinking any more of his destiny and the divine task he has undertaken. Dido for her part has no thoughts other than her love for Aeneas and her desire to keep him with her; she is persuaded by her sister Anna to break the vow she had made to the ashes of her dead husband Sychaeus, and she no longer cares for the well-being of Carthage; her city's activities grind to a halt (4.86–9). The goddesses Venus and Juno conspire together to arrange a 'marriage' between Dido and Aeneas as they shelter together in a cave; the supernatural powers of nature convince Dido that it is a real marriage; as the lightning flash seems to her to be the wedding torch, the Nymphs sing a bridal song, and Juno herself witnesses the 'marriage'. Following this rumour spreads abroad stories of their 'wedding', and causes Iarbas, one of Dido's suitors, to pray to Jupiter that this Trojan interloper be not permitted to win Dido's favour.

This causes Jupiter to intervene; he instructs his messenger Mercury to go to Aeneas and tell him that he is failing in his divine duty, in his mission to found a city which will bring the whole world under the sway of its laws. Mercury delivers the message and for the first time in the book our attention is concentrated not on Dido but Aeneas. Aeneas is aghast at this message from heaven – as well he might be, for it brings him to a realisation of his forgetfulness. His human weakness is here apparent: he had yielded to the temptation to stay when he should not have done so, and his failure here not only jeopardises his position as a willing servant of providence, but also leads directly to the death of Dido, who had been led to believe that Aeneas would stay.

Aeneas in this conflict between love and duty decides immediately for duty – 'he longs to get away and to leave the land he loves' (281); but where Virgil puts the emphasis is not on the triumph of the right, the victory of Rome over a dangerous obstacle, but on the suffering and death of Dido. She appeals to Aeneas to stay; he replies that he must against his will follow his divine mission. His speech is cold, deliberately so because he is afraid of being shaken in his resolve: 'because of the orders of Jupiter he kept his eyes unmoving and with a great struggle concealed the love in his heart' (331–2). He argues that he had not entered a marriage compact (which is true), and that he is forced by heaven's decrees to go to Italy; he tells her that Mercury has just appeared to tell him so. His arguments have no effect on Dido; realising that he intends to go she curses him and prays for vengeance. She collapses and is escorted away, and Aeneas is left alone. Virgil summarises his plight in four moving lines:

> at pius Aeneas, quamquam lenire dolentem
> solando cupit et dictis avertere curas,
> multa gemens magnoque animum labefactus amore
> iussa tamen divum exsequitur classemque revisit.
>
> (4.393–6)

But Aeneas listened to the call of duty, and although he longed to lighten her sorrow with consolation and to turn away her anguish with his words, groaning deeply and shaken to the heart by his deep love, nevertheless followed out the orders of the gods and went back to his fleet.

Nothing could more clearly reveal the conflict in the unhappy Aeneas: his devotion to his mission has prevailed over his personal wishes, his intellectual and moral decision has prevailed over his emotional agonies. The sacrifice is very great; Rome could only grow by the great sacrifices of her servants. Not every reader of *Aeneid* 4 perceives this, because Dido, whose sufferings end in tragedy, commands far more attention than Aeneas, who overcomes his sufferings; the extent and significance of our sympathy for Dido will be discussed in the next chapter, but what we must notice here is that Aeneas sacrifices his personal life for what divine voices tell him he must do for the good of his people and of the world.

Once the decision has been taken and he is no longer with Dido, Aeneas is able to resist all further pleas; 'the fates stand in the way, and the god blocks his mortal ears which would have listened' (440). In a memorable simile Virgil compares Aeneas with an oak tree, buffeted by the winds but holding firm in spite of all: 'his resolution remains unchanged, the tears fall in vain' (449).

The same night Mercury appears again to Aeneas and tells him to leave immediately, before Dido takes some action to stop him. The Trojan fleet sails, and Dido, calling curses upon Aeneas and all the Romans, kills herself.

Book 5

The Trojans are driven by a storm to the western shores of Sicily, where they land and pay religious ceremonies at the tomb of Anchises, the anniversary of whose death it is. They celebrate funeral games in his honour, and the majority of the book is taken up with a description of these. The emotional tension is greatly diminished, but tragedy strikes again when the Trojan women are persuaded by Juno to set fire to the ships to prevent further voyaging over unknown seas. This new blow reduces Aeneas to a state bordering on despair, and he prays to Jupiter either to quench the flames or to send his thunderbolt upon them to end everything. Aeneas is given his epithet *pius*, and he appeals to Jupiter's own *pietas* towards men.

> tum pius Aeneas umeris abscindere vestem
> auxilioque vocare deos et tendere palmas:
> 'Iuppiter omnipotens, si nondum exosus ad unum
> Troianos, si quid pietas antiqua labores
> respicit humanos, da flammam evadere classi
> nunc, pater, et tenuis Teucrum res eripe leto.
> vel tu, quod superest, infesto fulmine morti,
> si mereor, demitte tuaque hic obrue dextra.

(5.685–92)

Then Aeneas, man of god, tore his robe from his shoulders and called on the gods for help, holding out his upturned hands: 'Almighty Jupiter, if you do not yet hate the Trojans to a man, if your loving-kindness of old looks on mortal sufferings, grant the fleet to escape the fire, now, father Jupiter, and save the frail fortunes of the Trojans from destruction. Otherwise, the one thing left, cast me down to death with your deadly thunderbolt and overwhelm me with your right hand'.

Aeneas' prayer is answered, and the fire quenched, and all the ships saved except four. But the disaster has made him despondent and uncertain, and he reaches here his lowest ebb, actually wondering whether to 'forget the fates'.

> at pater Aeneas casu concussus acerbo
> nunc huc ingentis, nunc illuc pectore curas
> mutabat versans, Siculisne resideret arvis
> oblitus fatorum, Italasne capesseret oras.
>
> (5.700–3)

> But father Aeneas, deeply shaken at this bitter blow, pondered over his deep anxieties turning his thoughts in his heart one way and another: should he settle in the Sicilian fields, forgetting the fates, or keep on for the shores of Italy?

He listens to a consoling speech, full of Stoic phrases about endurance, from the old priest Nautes, but he is far from heartened; he continues to be racked by his worries and uncertainty. It is not until Jupiter sends him a vision of the ghost of his father Anchises confirming the suggestions of Nautes (to leave behind the weak and press onwards himself with the strong) that he is able to recover something of his strength and confidence. Anchises tells him to continue onwards to Italy and there to enter the underworld (by way of Lake Avernus near Cumae) and to meet with him in Elysium: there he promises that he will reveal to Aeneas the future destiny of his race. The ghost disappears and Aeneas first humbly performs worship to the gods; then he arranges to leave behind some of his people in Sicily, and himself departs with the rest for Italy. The significance of this episode is tremendous – here is a man sorely tried, buffeted by adverse fortune, scarcely able to continue, yet receiving, at the hour of imminent defeat, supernatural aid and strength. This is the point at which the mission is most nearly abandoned, and had Aeneas not been a man who could hear the divine voice and respond to it, the mission would indeed have been abandoned. Rome was founded by the heroic endeavours of its men with the assistance of divine aid given to those willing and worthy to receive it; and it was in this way that it cóuld achieve and maintain its greatness.

Book 6

This is the crucial book in the development of Aeneas' character and resolution. Everything that has gone before is summarised in it, and from it all the events of the rest of the poem take their starting point. At the beginning of his experiences in the underworld, and during the first two-thirds of the book Aeneas is still backward-looking, regretful, uncertain; but after his meeting with Anchises and the revelation of the future destiny of Rome he is strengthened and resolved to be successful in his mission.

Aeneas and the Sibyl (Vatican MS of Virgil: fourth century)

The first section of the book (1–263) describes the preliminaries to the descent. An atmosphere of supernatural awe is built up by the description of the Sibyl's prophetic frenzy, the search for the golden bough, the death of Misenus and the funeral ceremonies for him, the sacrifices preliminary to the descent. The formidable task awaiting Aeneas is grimly outlined by the Sibyl:

> o tandem magnis pelagi defuncte periclis
> (sed terrae graviora manent), in regna Lavini
> Dardanidae venient (mitte hanc de pectore curam),
> sed non et venisse volent. bella, horrida bella,
> et Thybrim multo spumantem sanguine cerno.

(6.83–7)

O you who have at last finished with the great perils of the sea (but worse await you on land), the Trojans shall come to their kingdom of Lavinium (so cast that anxiety from your heart), but they will wish that they had not come. I see wars, grim wars, and the Tiber foaming with torrents of blood.

She goes on to outline the opposition which Aeneas will meet, at the hands of mortal enemies and also through the continued opposition of Juno, and finally exhorts him: 'Do not yield to these troubles, but go the more boldly forward against them by whatever way your fortune permits it' (6.95–6). The reader wonders whether Aeneas will be able to muster the strength to do so.

Aeneas' reply, however, indicates his Stoic endurance, as he tells the Sibyl: 'No form of toil that presents itself to me is anything new or unexpected; I have thought it all over before, and gone through it all in my thoughts already.' He asks to be permitted to visit his father in the underworld; the Sibyl replies that to descend and return is granted to very few, but that if he finds and picks the golden bough he will be permitted to enter the realms of Pluto. Aided by his goddess mother Venus, Aeneas does so, and after the funeral celebrations for his friend Misenus he fulfils the appropriate sacrifices to the shades, and enters the underworld through the cave at Lake Avernus over which no birds fly.

The middle section of the book is presented in the form of a journey through the various parts of Pluto's realm as the Sibyl and Aeneas make their way towards Elysium where Anchises waits. Virgil uses the traditional geography of the underworld (the rivers with the ferryman, the dog Cerberus guarding the approach) as a setting for Aeneas' meeting with three of the ghosts of his past – Palinurus, Dido, Deiphobus. Aeneas had been closely involved with the death of each, and to each he speaks in tones of regret and personal remorse, still looking sorrowfully back upon the past rather than hopefully forward toward the future.

The first ghost Aeneas meets is that of his faithful helmsman Palinurus, swept overboard on the last stages of the journey from Sicily to Italy, and therefore unburied and forbidden to cross the Styx in Charon's boat.

Aeneas had been overcome with sorrow at the sight of all the unburied dead, thick as leaves falling in winter or birds migrating to warmer lands, and when he recognises Palinurus among them he blames Apollo for having broken his promise that Palinurus would safely reach Italy. Palinurus assures him that Apollo did not deceive him, for he swam to Italy but was killed on landing – he beseeches Aeneas for help, but Aeneas is powerless to give it.

The note of sorrow is even more dominant when Aeneas reaches the Fields of Mourning, the abode of those who died of unhappy love. Here he meets the ghost of Dido whose suicide when Aeneas left her is still fresh in the memory. We must pause on this passage, for it strongly emphasises what suffering Aeneas' mission had caused to both himself and Dido, and how he still cannot free himself from feelings of guilt and remorse about the past.

When Aeneas recognised Dido's ghost he wept and spoke to her in the sweet tones of love:

> infelix Dido, verus mihi nuntius ergo
> venerat exstinctam ferroque extrema secutam?
> funeris heu tibi causa fui? per sidera iuro,
> per superos et si qua fides tellure sub ima est,
> invitus, regina, tuo de litore cessi.
> sed me iussa deum, quae nunc has ire per umbras,
> per loca senta situ cogunt noctemque profundam,
> imperiis egere suis; nec credere quivi
> hunc tantum tibi me discessu ferre dolorem.
> siste gradum teque aspectu ne subtrahe nostro.
> quem fugis? extremum fato quod te adloquor hoc est.
>
> (6.456–66)

Unhappy Dido, then it was a true report that came to me, saying you were dead and had ended all with the sword? Alas, was I the cause of your death? By the stars I swear, by the gods above and any trust there is deep below the earth, unwillingly, O queen, I left your shores. But it was the orders of the gods, which now force me to travel through this land of shades, through ragged and forlorn places and deepest night, that drove me on with their commands – nor could I have believed that I was bringing you such great grief by my departure. Halt your steps and do not run away from my sight. Who are you running from? This is the last word, fate decrees it, which I may speak to you.

But Dido makes no response, standing motionless as if she were flint or marble; and finally she tears herself away and joins the ghost of her former husband Sychaeus. Aeneas, 'shaken by her unhappy fate, followed her far with tears in his eyes, pitying her as she went' (475–6).

In this passage, one of the most moving in the whole poem, we see the repetition by Aeneas of the reasons he had given to Dido in life to explain why he could not stay: he did not himself want to go, he insists, his personal decision would have been to stay with her, but he had to sacrifice all thoughts of self to the orders of the gods. Duty had to prevail over love, and at what a cost.

The other point of enormous significance here is that Aeneas is filled with guilt and remorse and sorrow over the disasters of the past. Though he knows intellectually that he has done the right thing, it gives him no satisfaction; he weeps and pities Dido, his thoughts are still in the sorrowful past. But what he has to learn, and what she teaches him now, is that the past is dead: nothing can alter it, there is no point in brooding over it. By her total rejection of him she makes it easier for him to learn this hard lesson. He will not ever forget her – how could he? – but he must accept that he must live for the future, not for the silent past.

The third ghost Aeneas meets is that of his comrade-in-arms, Deiphobus, and the effect upon him is similar to that of Dido. He feels guilt for having failed to help Deiphobus when he was killed on Troy's last night, for having himself escaped alive when Deiphobus and so many others died. But Deiphobus tells him not to blame himself, and as they part says to him

i decus, i, nostrum; melioribus utere fatis.

Forward, glory of our race, forward; enjoy happier fate in the future.

This is the essence of what Aeneas has learned: his thoughts must turn forwards and not backwards, and by means of the reliving of three crucial episodes of his past life, he is finally freed from them, and ready to go forward.

In the last part of the book Aeneas reaches Elysium, meets his father Anchises and learns more of the glorious future awaiting him. He has learned that he must leave the past behind; now he is given the resolution and confidence to face the future with joy and hope. Anchises greets him by saying:

venisti tandem, tuaque exspectata parenti
vicit iter durum pietas?   (687–8)

Have you come at last, and has your devotion to duty, awaited by your father, prevailed on your hard road?

This sums up the story of the first half of the poem: it is devotion to duty that has prevailed – by a narrow margin – and the road had indeed been hard. 'How much I feared', Anchises adds, 'that the realm of Libya [Dido's realm] might cause you harm.' Yes, indeed.

Now Anchises reveals to Aeneas the pageant of Roman heroes waiting to be born if Aeneas succeeds in his mission in founding his city (this passage has been analysed on pp. 17f.); and after the high point of the pageant, the description of the future emperor Augustus, he breaks off to ask his son this significant question:

> et dubitamus adhuc virtutem extendere factis,
> aut metus Ausonia prohibet consistere terra? (806–7)

> And do we still hesitate to enlarge our prowess by deeds, or does fear prevent us from settling in Italian land?

Aeneas did not reply, but we can reply for him – there will be no more hesitation now. And when the pageant is concluded Anchises has 'fired Aeneas' heart with love for the glory to come' (889). He has passed from passive, almost reluctant, acceptance of a mission that seemed often too heavy for him and whose real nature he did not understand to a positive active love for his task.

Books 7–12

Virgil's presentation of Aeneas' character in the first half of the *Aeneid* has revealed the psychological conflicts, the inner battles which had to be fought and won before the foundation of Rome could be achieved. The second half shows a different kind of character study of the new hero. We know now that he will have the strength to prevail – the problem now is, how will he do it? How will he overcome the physical obstacles of opposition and warfare? How does the hero behave when he knows that what he must do is for the good of the world, but he comes up against people who do not accept it? Does he prevail by clemency? By negotiation? By violence? This is the question which Virgil explores throughout the last six books, finding no easy answer, but seeking to define, in one situation after another, what kind of behaviour seems appropriate for the prototype of a ruler of the Roman Empire.

Book 7

Near the beginning of the second half of his poem Virgil invokes the Muse again to tell him of the battles to be fought (*horrida bella*), and says that a greater succession of events rises up before him, and he undertakes

D

a greater work (*maius opus moveo*). Most readers find the first half of the poem more interesting than the second, and it is worth pausing for a moment to consider why Virgil says that the second half is more important (for this I think is what his phrase implies). The question can be answered on several levels; simply that from the preparations Virgil turns now to the achievement; or that from foreign countries he now turns to describe events in his own Italy; or that Homer's *Iliad* was regarded generally as greater than his *Odyssey* (*Aeneid* 7–12 resemble the *Iliad*, while *Aeneid* 1–6 are like the *Odyssey*). But any or all of these seem insufficient; it is perhaps rather that Virgil now comes to the consideration of how a worthy object (civilisation for the world) is to be achieved when it runs up against opposition. Virgil, like any Roman of his time, was enough of a realist to know that opposition would exist; historically it had existed throughout the whole period of Rome's rise to power, and had often involved violence. In the story of Rome's first founder this realistic state of affairs had to be presented; we see early in Book 7 that there were some who wanted to accept Aeneas peacefully, but others who did not. Virgil's problem was to try to define the best method of countering violence (the word *violentia* is used of Turnus and of no one else in the poem). He sets out to show Aeneas fighting only because he must, aiming to end it as mercifully as possible and establish a lasting peace. As will be seen, Aeneas does not succeed always in satisfying us that he can do this; he is sometimes, under provocation, ruthless and savage. But what is important is that Virgil has explored in situation after situation the pressures and ambitions and aspirations of men seeking victory, and enlarged the vision of the Romans and succeeding generations about the nature of conflict.

The seventh book begins serenely and optimistically, and it seems at first as though Aeneas will succeed in his dearest wish, to achieve his destiny without bloodshed. King Latinus welcomes the Trojans hospitably, and when he hears from Ilioneus that the fates have brought the Trojans to the river Tiber by the instructions of heaven, he recognises the fulfilment of an oracle that the princess Lavinia is to marry a stranger, and he sends gifts to Aeneas as a token that he will receive the Trojans in peace. But this happy situation is immediately destroyed by Juno, who summons up the fiend Allecto from the underworld to enrage Queen Amata and Turnus, the Rutulian leader who is already betrothed to Lavinia. Allecto symbolises the fury in human beings which causes them to profane peace (line 467), and she can only act upon Amata and Turnus because they are the kind of people liable to feelings of fury. Yet – and here is the focus of our interest in Virgil's treatment of the story – both have much to be said on their side, both have reason for fury. Amata wishes Turnus to be her son-in-law, and Turnus wishes to marry Lavinia and sees no reason to be pushed aside by a foreign invader (oracle or no oracle). Many have seen in the brave, forthright, impetuous Turnus the true hero of the poem; but this is a wholly mistaken view. Whatever may be said for Turnus, he is portrayed as too ready to leap to arms, too fond of fighting; this, as we shall see, is a major point of difference between him and Aeneas.

As a result of Allecto's intervention war begins, and the book ends with a catalogue of the brave Italian forces who went to war against Aeneas. Virgil makes no attempt to blacken the Italians because they are the enemy; rather they are treated with sympathy and admiration, and the prospect of war between them and the Trojans is shown to be senseless and pathetic (in a way almost an anticipation of Rome's civil wars), yet now (because of Allecto) unavoidable.

Book 8

How then is Aeneas to deal with the armed opposition? He does not rush straight in to combat; the first that we hear of him, now that war has begun, is his anxiety.

> magno curarum fluctuat aestu,
> atque animum nunc huc celerem nunc dividit illuc
> in partisque rapit varias perque omnia versat,
> sicut aquae tremulum labris ubi lumen aenis
> sole repercussum aut radiantis imagine lunae
> omnia pervolitat late loca, iamque sub auras
> erigitur summique ferit laquearia tecti.
>
> (8.19–25)

He tosses on a great sea of anxieties, and shoots his swift thoughts one way and another, rapidly directing them towards all kinds of aspects, turning them through all possibilities. Like flickering light reflected off the water in bronze vessels from the sun or the form of the shining moon, when it flits all around everywhere, rising up now to the heights and catching the gilt panels in the high ceiling.

Night falls, and all other creatures were enjoying deep slumber before Aeneas at last lay down to rest, 'disturbed in his heart by the grim war' (29). We see a picture of the rational hero, disturbed at the situation and pondering his best course of action – very much the opposite of the impetuous Turnus. As he sleeps the river-god Tiber appears to him, taking away his worries (35) with a heartening speech, telling him that he has indeed arrived at the site of his new city and that he must go for help to the Arcadian king Evander, at his city Pallanteum, a little way up the Tiber on the site where one day Rome will be built.

The rest of the eighth book is a peaceful account of Aeneas' visit to the site of the future Rome and of the making of new armour for him by Vulcan at Venus' instigation. There is no warfare in this book, and we see Aeneas in a context of friendship. He marvels at the beauty of Evander's little city, and he is told of the reasons for the sacrifices to Hercules then taking place. This is a prototype of the famous Roman festival in Hercules' honour at the *Ara Maxima*, and Virgil dwells on it at length, thus establishing a strong religious basis for Aeneas' conversation with Evander (both men are seen to be deeply religious) and also linking with Roman Stoicism. Hercules was a patron deity of the Stoic philosophy, being a type of strength against adversity and furthering the advance of civilisation by the removal from the world of various monsters. The story told in Book 8 about his defeat of the fire-breathing monster Cacus exemplifies this, and so do various references through the poem to Hercules and his deeds (e.g. 6.285 ff., the monsters at the portal of Hell, 6.801 ff..). In a sense Aeneas has to be a new Hercules, a man who for his deeds to improve man's civilisation was destined for deification; and the same is true in a sense of Augustus too, who is compared with Hercules in 6.801 ff.

It is perhaps in Book 8 that Aeneas is most truly himself.

Book 9

Aeneas plays no part in the events of the ninth book, which take place at the Trojan camp during his absence with King Evander. But the nature of his responsibility is made very clear, as during his absence disaster after disaster comes upon his men, and Turnus is able actually to breach the defence walls. The military bravery and leadership of Aeneas is very sadly missed.

Book 10

The return of Aeneas with his allies, by sea, is presented by Virgil in very vivid colours. As he comes in sight of his camp he raises his great shield aloft, and the light shines from his armour like a comet or like the star Sirius (270 f.), boding ill for his enemies. This is reminiscent of the picture of Augustus at Actium (8.678 f.); each of them is majestic, frightening, righteous as he moves to confront his enemies.

The battle develops; the opposing leaders, Turnus and Aeneas, each achieve great deeds. The narrative shifts to the young Pallas, sent by

Evander to help Aeneas. He faces Lausus, son of Mezentius, but Turnus sees him and calls on his allies to leave Pallas to him. The episode which follows is of crucial importance to the *Aeneid* and to Aeneas himself: Turnus ruthlessly and cruelly kills Pallas, thus providing the reason for his own death at the hands of Aeneas, who would have spared him after victory, had it not been for this. The crucial question we have to ask ourselves at the end of the *Aeneid* is whether Aeneas was justified in killing Turnus when he begged for mercy; the reason why he does not spare him is because he wants to take vengeance for Pallas. We must therefore examine this episode closely, asking ourselves whether Turnus' behaviour is such that we can approve Aeneas' later act of vengeance in killing him.

Turnus, when he sees Pallas, cries out:

> tempus desistere pugnae;
> solus ego in Pallanta feror, soli mihi Pallas
> debetur; cuperem ipse parens spectator adesset.
>
> (10.441-3)

> It is time for you to rest from battle: I and I only am going to deal with Pallas, to me and me only is he due – I wish his father were here to see it.

Hard words, and cruel, and such as to turn sympathy away from Turnus, however much one accepts that it is his job to defeat the enemy, and that if he does not kill Pallas, Pallas will kill him. Pallas throws his spear first unavailingly; then Turnus hurls his, saying 'See whether my spear reaches its mark better', and Pallas is mortally wounded. Turnus standing over him speaks these words:

> Arcades, haec, inquit, memores mea dicta referte
> Euandro; qualem meruit, Pallanta remitto.
>
> (10.491-2)

> 'Arcadians, remember to take these words of mine to Evander: I send him Pallas back as he deserves to have him.'

Then he strips him of his sword-belt, rejoicing in the spoils. Now Virgil enters the narrative in his own person to comment:

> nescia mens hominum fati sortisque futurae
> et servare modum rebus sublata secundis!
> Turno tempus erit magno cum optaverit emptum
> intactum Pallanta, et cum spolia ista diemque
> oderit.
>
> (10.501-5)

How unaware are men's minds of fate and their future fortune, and of how to show moderation when uplifted by success! There will be a time for Turnus when he would give anything not to have touched Pallas, and when he will look back with loathing on this day and the spoils he took.

Here the ending of the poem is anticipated, when Aeneas was about to spare the wounded Turnus, but when he saw him wearing the sword-belt he had stripped from Pallas, he changed his mind and killed him.

The news reaches Aeneas, and for the first time since he left Troy we see him enraged, indeed berserk. His constant efforts to control the irrational elements in himself here break down: he yields to fury. Is he right to do so? Under this provocation one might perhaps think so; but Virgil disquiets us by presenting Aeneas' fury in the strongest possible terms. 'He hacks down with the sword everything in his path, in his hot anger cutting a broad path through the enemy line as he seeks you, Turnus, as you exult in your recent slaughter' (513 f.). Aeneas then takes eight captives alive to be sacrificed at the funeral of Pallas. This piece of barbarity is very startling indeed: to such a point can the most rational and considerate of military leaders descend under the pressure of battle frenzy and vengeance. The passage is based on one in Homer where Achilles, in his wild sorrow for the death of Patroclus, makes human sacrifice at his tomb; it is startling and horrible in Homer, but very much more so in the gentle Virgil. In Homer war is seen as part of the inevitable condition of man, yet atrocities such as this are nevertheless horrifying; but in Virgil war is seen as an evil which one day will pass away in the march of civilisation, and this kind of barbarity leads the reader to doubt whether human endeavour will ever rise superior to the evils of violence.

Aeneas' behaviour continues to be violent in the extreme: Magus begs for mercy and offers ransom, beseeching Aeneas by his father and young son, but Aeneas replies that all such possibilities have been removed by Turnus killing Pallas. This, he says bitterly, my father and my son would approve; and he kills the suppliant. Next he kills the priest Haemonides, and then Tarquitus, kicking his prostrate body, and telling him his body will be food for vultures or fishes. Many others he kills, 'raging victorious over the plain when once his sword had tasted blood' (569 f.). Next to meet him is Lucagus; he kills him and sarcastically boasts over him (591 ff.), and when his brother Liger begs for mercy Aeneas taunts him: 'die and do not be separated from your brother' (600). Virgil summarises this section thus: 'These were the men Aeneas killed on the battlefield, raging like a torrent or a black whirlwind' (602-4). The word *furens* ('raging') is the word constantly used in the poem of the irrational kind of human behaviour which man must strive to overcome.

The narrative now turns away from the battlefield to Olympus, and when we next hear of Aeneas he is attacking Mezentius (769); he wounds him and Mezentius' young son Lausus intervenes to save his father. He ignores Aeneas' warning and is killed. Then at last a revulsion of feeling sweeps over Aeneas – from hot joy in battle he turns in an instant to sorrow. 'He groaned deeply in pity, and held out his hand and there came into his mind the thought of his own love for his father.' He speaks to the dead man in tones of pity, does not strip him of his armour, and promises to return his body to his family. Obviously there is a comparison to be made here with Turnus' behaviour towards Pallas, and it is entirely in Aeneas' favour. This is the sort of man we have been led to believe that the hero of the poem will be, and for the most part this is indeed the kind of man he is. But he was not like it immediately after the death of Pallas, and we shall see that in the twelfth book he reverts again to wild fury. Two questions may be put: the first is 'Can Aeneas or his sons, or his sons' sons, gradually become better at controlling their wild fury?'; and the second is much deeper – 'Should men in the Roman world in every conceivable situation control their wild fury, or are there times when they should give it free rein?' If so, what are those times? Nothing could have been easier than for Virgil to avoid this dilemma, and to present Aeneas only in situations where he did and could show total self-control; but it was precisely this dilemma that Virgil insisted on confronting.

Book 11

The feelings of pity and sorrow which the death of Lausus induced in Aeneas are continued very powerfully indeed in the opening scenes of the eleventh book, as Virgil describes the funeral of Pallas. Here we see Aeneas showing his anguish at the suffering involved in war, organising the last rites for the dead boy in a passage where the echoes of the lyric poet Catullus emphasise the intensity of grief. He ends by saying:

> nos alias hinc ad lacrimas eadem horrida belli
> fata vocant: salve aeternum mihi, maxime Palla,
> aeternumque vale. (11.96–8)

> The same grim fates of war call us away to other tears: hail for ever, mightiest Pallas, and for ever farewell.

Envoys come from the Latins asking for a truce to bury the dead, and Aeneas immediately grants it, saying:

> pacem me exanimis et Martis sorte peremptis
> oratis? equidem et vivis concedere vellem. (110–11)

Do you ask me for peace for the dead, those taken off by the fortunes of war? I would indeed gladly have granted it to the living too.

These are expressions very far distant from those he had used to the warriors who begged him for mercy after the death of Pallas.

Aeneas goes on to emphasise that he does not wish to fight and has no personal desire for glory: 'I would not have come', he says, 'had not fate appointed this place for me to settle in; I do not wage war with the people. Turnus has persuaded King Latinus to reject the alliance he made with me; Turnus ought to settle the war by fighting me in single combat' (112–15).

The rest of the book is mainly taken up with an account of the fighting, especially of the death of Turnus' ally, the warrior maiden Camilla, and at the beginning of the last book Turnus sees that he must now himself face Aeneas.

Book 12

As we come to the decisive moment of the conflict between Turnus and Aeneas, it will be useful to pause for a moment to summarise the difference between their characters. Turnus is in every way a Homeric hero, possessing the outlook and character of an Achilles (with whom he was equated by the Sibyl, 6.89). He is impetuous, energetic, ruthless, violent; he represents personal prowess, irresponsible individuality in contrast with the public and social virtues which Aeneas shows, or seeks to show. He represents, to use Horace's phrases from *Odes* 3.4.65–6, *vis consili expers* (strength without wisdom) in contrast to the *vis temperata* (controlled strength) of Aeneas. He fights for his own glory and reputation; Aeneas fights because he must, in the bitter fulfilment of duty. He fights what the Romans would call a 'bellum iustum', a 'just war', and Turnus does not. These generalisations have already been illustrated from situations in the poem, and they can be reinforced by a study of the words used of each in the poem. Words used of Turnus and not of Aeneas are *violentia* ('violence'), *audax* ('bold'), *fiducia* ('self-confidence'), *insania* ('madness'), *turbidus* ('wild'), *superbus* ('proud'); words used more often of Turnus than Aeneas include *ardens* ('burning'), *furens* ('frenzied'), *ira* ('anger'). Words used of Aeneas and not of Turnus are – first and foremost of course *pius* and *pietas* ('devotion to duty'); *iustitia* ('justice'), *bonus* ('good'). The use of similes reinforces the picture: Aeneas is hardly ever compared with a wild animal (he and his followers are like wolves in Book 2 and Aeneas is like a bull in 12), while Turnus is compared three times with a lion, twice with a bull, twice with a wolf, and once with an eagle and a tiger. Finally the emblem on Turnus' helmet (7.785 f.) is a chimaera, an archaic monster, which belches forth fire which grows hotter as the battle becomes fiercer; this symbolises the archaic and barbaric energy of this survival of the heroic world which Aeneas seeks to leave behind.

Now as we have seen there are two qualifications to be made to the theme of the previous paragraph: one is that for all his violence there is something noble and splendid about Turnus, and the other is that for all his attempts to pursue the social virtues Aeneas sometimes falls into violence. But broadly and on the whole it is true that Turnus cares primarily for himself and Aeneas primarily for others.

We see the real Turnus at the beginning of Book 12: when he sees that everyone is looking to him, then like a wounded lion he rouses himself for defiance – he is on fire and violence possesses him (9). He proclaims that he accepts the single combat; when Latinus and Amata attempt to dissuade him at first he can hardly speak, and when the words tumble out they convey his impetuous passion to put himself to the ultimate test. He welcomes the opportunity to fight for his honour, he seizes the chance of the heroic gesture. He arms for battle – Virgil gives a long description of this (82 ff.) – and his eyes sparkle in anticipation (101 ff.). Battle is his business.

Arrangements are made between Latinus and Aeneas for the single combat, and Aeneas promises that if he loses he will withdraw; if he wins he will not subjugate the Italians and he seeks no empires for himself – the two peoples will be linked together for ever under equal laws. Aeneas' moderation and statesmanlike attitude is seen here at its clearest; he is always at his most admirable in formal situations where the clashing elements of personality can most easily be subdued.

The Rutulians are unhappy, as well they might be, that Turnus must fight for them all against so formidable an opponent, and they break the truce. Again we see Aeneas at his most admirable: he rushes out with head bare holding out his hands to restrain his men:

> quo ruitis? quaeve ista repens discordia surgit?
> o cohibete iras! ictum iam foedus et omnes
> compositae leges, mihi ius concurrere soli,
> me sinite atque auferte metus.

(12.313–6)

Where are you rushing to? What is this sudden tumult rising up? Oh control your anger! The treaty is already made and all its clauses agreed. It is right for me alone to meet him; leave it to me and away with your fears.

But as he speaks he is struck by an arrow, and has to withdraw from the battlefield; the wound is healed by Venus, and he returns to the fight. His deeds and those of Turnus are described side by side, and there is no difference between them. Under the anger caused by his wound Aeneas reverts to the violence of the battlefield, and fights like any Homeric hero.

The Trojans are successful in the fighting, and again Turnus prepares to meet Aeneas. Frequently in the events of the single combat we are reminded of the combat between Achilles and Hector told in *Iliad* 22, when Achilles chased Hector round the walls of Troy and caught and killed him: Jupiter weighs the fates of the opponents in the scales (*Aeneid* 12.725 ff., *Iliad* 22.209 ff.); Aeneas pursues Turnus as a hound pursues a stag (*Aeneid* 12.749 ff., *Iliad* 22.188 ff.); the onlookers are prevented from joining in (*Aeneid* 12.760 ff., *Iliad* 22.205 ff.); the chase continued round the walls, not for a prize in the games, but for the life of the loser (*Aeneid* 12.763 ff., *Iliad* 22.158 ff.); eventually the loser becomes like a man in a dream (*Aeneid* 12.908 ff., *Iliad* 22.199 ff.); finally the loser begs for mercy (*Aeneid* 12.930 ff., *Iliad* 22.338 ff.); he is not granted it, because (in the *Iliad*) he has killed Patroclus, because (in the *Aeneid*) he has killed Pallas. Turnus then is the Achilles figure who this time does not win; Aeneas is the Hector figure who this time wins.

We expect the new hero to act differently from the old in the moment of triumph; when Achilles had Hector in his power he refused all mercy and in a speech of arrogance and hatred alienated our sympathy from him. Aeneas surely, we feel, will behave differently; but we are wrong – he kills Turnus in a wave of anger and desire for vengeance. We must look at the passage in detail:

> ille humilis supplexque oculos dextramque precantem
> protendens 'equidem merui nec deprecor' inquit;
> 'utere sorte tua. miseri te si qua parentis
> tangere cura potest, oro (fuit et tibi talis
> Anchises genitor) Dauni miserere senectae
> et me, seu corpus spoliatum lumine mavis,
> redde meis. vicisti et victum tendere palmas
> Ausonii videre; tua est Lavinia coniunx,
> ulterius ne tende odiis.' stetit acer in armis
> Aeneas volvens oculos dextramque repressit;
> et iam iamque magis cunctantem flectere sermo
> coeperat, infelix umero cum apparuit alto

balteus et notis fulserunt cingula bullis
Pallantis pueri, victum quem vulnere Turnus
straverat atque umeris inimicum insigne gerebat.
ille, oculis postquam saevi monimenta doloris
exuviasque hausit, furiis accensus et ira
terribilis: 'tune hinc spoliis indute meorum
eripiare mihi? Pallas te hoc vulnere, Pallas
immolat et poenam scelerato ex sanguine sumit.'
hoc dicens ferrum adverso sub pectore condit
fervidus. ast illi solvuntur frigore membra
vitaque cum gemitu fugit indignata sub umbras.

(12.930–52)

Turnus, humbled, turned his eyes to Aeneas and held his right hand
out in prayer as a suppliant, and said: 'I have deserved it, and I
do not complain – use your good fortune. If any thought of my poor
father can touch you then I beg you (for you had such a father too,
Anchises) pity the old age of my father Daunus and send me – or if
you prefer my despoiled body – back to my people. You have won,
and the Italians have seen me defeated and stretching out my hands
to you; Lavinia is yours to wed; go no further in hatred.' Aeneas
fierce in his panoply stood still, shifting his gaze, and checked his
right hand; and Turnus' words began to move him more and more
as he hesitated, when the ill-starred sword-belt struck his eyes high
on Turnus' shoulder; the baldrick that had belonged to the young
Pallas with the studs he knew so well shone out, Pallas whom Turnus
had conquered with a fatal wound and laid low, and now was wearing
his foeman's emblem on his shoulder. Aeneas when he had gazed
long on the spoils that reminded him of his savage agony, set on
fire with frenzy and terrible in his anger said 'Are you going to be
saved from me here, wearing the spoils of my own people? It is
Pallas, Pallas I tell you, who sacrifices you with this blow, and
exacts punishment from your accursed blood.' As he said this he
buried his sword deep in his heart as he faced him, in hot anger;
but Turnus' limbs were loosened in the cold of death, and his life
with a groan fled complaining to the shades below.

The first thing that the reader feels here is sympathy for Turnus and regret
for Aeneas' action; notice that the very last line of the poem (this poem of
the destiny of Rome) is not about Aeneas or Rome at all, but about the
victim of Rome, the young Turnus whose life flies complaining to the
underworld. Small wonder in a sense that the pious readers of the Middle
Ages felt that Aeneas had not received the rewards due to him for his
success and that one Maphaeus Vegius in the fifteenth century wrote the
thirteenth book of the *Aeneid* in which the attention was focused on
Aeneas and his achievement, and the Trojan hero was duly received as a
god in heaven.

But that is not the way that Virgil has left it: Aeneas has failed to show the control and clemency which we expected of him. If it is argued that in this situation he cannot do otherwise, then it should be noticed that nothing could have been easier than for Virgil to avoid the situation. Turnus could have been killed, not wounded; then the question of clemency need not have arisen. It is quite plain that Virgil has deliberately ended with this dilemma – what does a man do under these stresses? And does he do what he should? Do we applaud or groan?

We must examine possible justifications. It could be said that Turnus represents a barbaric and antique way of life which can have no part in the new civilisation. It could be said that it is Rome's mission to 'cast down the proud' (*debellare superbos*), and Turnus is one of the *superbi*. There is clearly something in this, but Virgil has not emphasised this aspect: indeed the passage opens with Turnus described as 'humbled' (*humilis*).

The justification which Virgil has emphasised is the death of Pallas at Turnus' hands. We have already seen that the circumstances of this were such as to cause the reader to feel that Turnus deserved punishment, and this is in fact what Aeneas says – it is Pallas who inflicts the death wound. He kills him then in anger (*fervidus*), and out of vengeance. Are we to think that at the end after all his efforts to define a better way of life Aeneas has failed? Or are we to think that this is righteous anger, necessary to redress the wrongs of the past? Through the poem Aeneas has struggled to control frenzy and anger in himself and others; now he kills Turnus *furiis accensus et ira terribilis* ('set on fire with frenzy and terrible in his anger'). Through the centuries readers of Virgil have reacted in different ways to the ending of the poem; each reader must decide for himself whether Aeneas has acted rightly or not. What is certain is that Virgil's presentation of this dilemma sheds light on the eternal problems of the human condition.

Thus the character of Virgil's new type of hero is complex. For most of the time we admire him; but under the pressure of his own human nature he sometimes alienates, or partially alienates, our sympathy – as when he leaves Dido, when he goes berserk on the battlefield, when he kills Turnus. What is so fascinating about Aeneas in the poem is that he has his faults as well as his strengths, he has inner contradictions in his character which he attempts to resolve, sometimes successfully, sometimes not. He has a relationship with the gods but he remains human; in his journey through life he is sorely tested and sometimes fails, yet he keeps going; and in the end, against all the odds, and not always in the way he would have wished, he fulfils what he felt himself called on to do.

4

Virgil's private voice:
Dido, Turnus, Juno

WE have in Chapter 2 listened to the public voice of Virgil extolling the hopes and ideals of Rome's mission for world civilisation; we have seen in Chapter 3 how Aeneas attempted to define in his own life the nature of this new civilisation, with only partial success; we come now to the elements in the poem which seem to modify or contradict the public optimism of Rome's Golden Age.

The *Aeneid* is no unthinking panegyric; if it had been, Dido and Turnus, the main opponents of the Roman mission, would have been portrayed as hateful characters. So far is this from being true that many have felt that the events of Book 4 'break the back of the poem' (in the sense that our sympathy for Dido is so profound that we tend to reject the Roman mission), and many too that Turnus wins our admiration at the end. These two are individuals who are in opposition to fate and the Roman order; they are minorities who are trampled over by the great Roman juggernaut. Dido is an individual who cares nothing for Rome or the world issues involved, but wishes simply to win the man she loves; and she is prevented from winning her happiness not by the man himself (who would have wished to stay with her) but by the large-scale cosmic destiny of Rome. As an individual she can do nothing; her happiness is unimportant in the world plan – yet every reader of Book 4 feels that it is unjust that it should be so. Again Turnus must be brushed aside by the march of events – he does not belong to destiny and he must pay for that. His cause is in his eyes wholly just – to resist the invader who wishes to steal his bride; but because the march of destiny is in a different direction, his happiness and his life must be sacrificed. And besides Dido and Turnus there are countless others on both sides who lose their lives because of Rome's destiny. There are Euryalus and Nisus, Pallas and Lausus; and there are many of lesser fame, such as Aeolus:

> hic tibi mortis erant metae, domus alta sub Ida,
> Lyrnesi domus alta, solo Laurente sepulcrum.

(12.546–7)

Here was your bourne of death – your lofty home was beneath Mt Ida, at Lyrnesus your lofty home, but your tomb on Laurentian soil.

And others too, not named or counted:

> cetera confusaeque ingentem caedis acervum
> nec numero nec honore cremant.
>
> (11.207–8)

The rest, a great pile of mingled dead bodies, they burn uncounted and unsung.

It is the tension between Virgil's public voice and his private voice which makes the *Aeneid* the great poem that it is. Few poets of any age have been able to sympathise with both sides to the same extent: Virgil was moved by the great vision of Rome's destiny, yet he saw some of the unhappy implications; he sympathised deeply with private sorrow, yet he still admired the Roman national programme. Our eighteenth century admired him for his national note, for his patriotic message, the Victorians admired him for his tears for the lonely individual. T. S. Eliot admired him for his positive moral and ethical message of Rome; Robert Graves has criticised him as being too much a spokesman of the Roman government; most twentieth-century critics have praised him for his sensitivity to sorrow. It is the many-sidedness of the poem that makes it great: lovers of the established order can see in it a plea for order; rebels against the establishment can see in it a case for the outsider. What both these groups should see is that Virgil sympathises with both and criticises both. Just as Socrates the rationalist had his mystical side, so Virgil, the spokesman of Rome, recognises that there are other important things in the world as well as Roman imperialism.

We may transfer this conflict between Virgil's public voice and his private voice into a literary context. We could say that the public voice of Virgil is that of Ennius, Rome's first great national poet, of Cicero, especially of Livy as revealed again and again in the praises of the old Roman character which he presents in his history. The private voice of Virgil is like the voice of Catullus, poet of the individual and his joys and sorrows, who cared little for politics or the achievements of Julius Caesar or the mouthings of statesmen, but only for the reality of his private life in the little group of his personal friends. For Catullus affairs of state were nothing; reality was in his own personal experience and his own joys and sorrows and those of his friends. Ennius is recalled and imitated far more often in the *Aeneid* than Catullus – but when Catullus is recalled it is almost always in the most moving passages of the poem. At the death of

Euryalus, Catullus is echoed with a flower simile; at the funeral of Pallas he is recalled several times; but above all he is recalled in the tragedy of Dido in Book 4.

Catullus' poem on the marriage of Peleus and Thetis (poem 64) contains a long description of the desertion of Ariadne by Theseus. She had helped him to kill the Minotaur, thus incurring the wrath of her parents, and she runs away with him: they stay on the island of Dia and in the morning Ariadne wakes to find Theseus gone. Catullus paints a most moving picture of the loneliness and helplessness of the deserted princess, and her soliloquy as she gazes over the empty waves is filled with the sorrow and pathos which Catullus so often expressed in his lyrics. Virgil's Dido, while very different in many ways, resembles Ariadne in the pathos of desertion, and when she pleads with Aeneas not to leave her (4.305 ff.) her speech recalls that of Ariadne as she reproaches him with broken faith, promised marriage, ingratitude. Later in the book, as Dido speaks her last words (657–8), she uses the phrases of Catullus' Ariadne as she says:

> felix, heu nimium felix, si litora tantum
> numquam Dardaniae tetigissent nostra carinae.

> Happy, oh all too happy I would have been if only the Trojan ships had never touched our shores.

The story of Dido's tragedy has always been the best known part of the whole *Aeneid*; this was true already in Ovid's time (*Trist.* 2.533 ff.) and has remained true ever since. In Chaucer's *House of Fame* Dido has twice as much space as all the rest of the *Aeneid*; tragedies on the theme were frequently written (for example Marlowe's *Dido Queen of Carthage*); of musical treatments Purcell's opera is well known; Walter Savage Landor represented the feelings of many Victorians when he said that there was nothing so sublime and impassioned in literature as the tragedy of Dido in *Aeneid* 4. It has been said that Dido is the only character created by a Roman poet to pass into world literature (unlike most other famous characters of classical poetry she does not figure in Greek literature).

Thus we have the paradox that the most un-Roman part of Virgil's epic of Rome is the best known part. The point does not need elaborating further: it would be difficult not to be moved to pity and sympathy for Dido. Why has Virgil done this, and so damaged our confidence in the validity of Rome's mission by making us sympathise so much with the person who tries to prevent it from coming true? Nothing could have been easier than so to portray Dido that when Aeneas got out of her clutches a feeling of relief and triumph could have been established. She could have been modelled on the witches in Homer's *Odyssey*, Circe and Calypso, or the

Sirens, who try to prevent the homecoming of Odysseus and whose failure to do so leaves us with a feeling not of sympathy for them but of admiration for Odysseus. There was too a special historical reason why Dido could have been presented like this; she was a Carthaginian, and in Rome's long history it was the state of Carthage which had come closest of all to destroying Rome and her mission, especially during the Second Punic War at the end of the third century BC when Hannibal crossed the Alps and seemed to have Rome in his power.

There were all these reasons then why Dido could have been presented unsympathetically, and we may hazard a guess (though it will only be a guess) that when Virgil first sketched out the plot of his poem he did not intend that Dido should win such sympathy. It was when he came to compose her story that he felt increasingly the pathos of the defeated, that he saw Dido's rejection not from Rome's point of view but from Dido's.

But when all has been said about our sympathy for Dido – and much more could be said, and indeed often has been said by those who have written about the *Aeneid* – it is right that we should finally look again at the other side. Intellectually we must approve of Aeneas' decision to leave. When Mercury comes to him to remind him of his destiny he recognises that he has been at fault and he immediately takes his decision for Rome. Against the pathos of Dido's pleas he stands firm with the resolution of duty, and as she turns from pleas to threats and curses he still stands firm. He has the will to prefer the future to the present.

Turnus in many essentials resembles Dido. In the structure of the poem he constitutes an obstacle to the divine will which must be overcome – yet when he is overcome there is powerful sympathy for him and a feeling of injustice. Many have seen in him the real hero of the poem (perhaps rather as William Blake suggested that in *Paradise Lost* Milton was 'of the Devil's party without knowing it'; it is very noticeable that in Milton some of Satan's traits and acts are based on Virgil's Turnus). Above all Turnus, like Dido, is shown not as an impersonal 'obstacle' but as a real human character. We have already discussed his youthful impetuosity, his energy, his bravery; we may now look at the way in which (in Book 12) Virgil shows his human qualities in the hour of his ultimate test. After the arrangements have been made for the single combat Turnus momentarily loses his impetuous self-confidence: the Rutulians feel that the conquest is unequal, and this feeling is heightened by Turnus' humble demeanour:

adiuvat incessu tacito progressus et aram
suppliciter venerans demisso lumine Turnus
pubentesque genae et iuvenali in corpore pallor.

(12.219–21)

Turnus increased this feeling as he came forward without speaking and worshipped at the altar humbly, with downcast gaze; his face was so youthful and all his young body so pale.

Again as the moment for facing Aeneas approaches Turnus realises, as Hector had done when facing Achilles (Homer, *Iliad* 22.300 ff.), that the gods are against him, and he now shows the same courage in facing death:

> terga dabo et Turnum fugientem haec terra videbit?
> usque adeone mori miserum est? vos o mihi, Manes,
> este boni, quoniam superis aversa voluntas.
> sancta ad vos anima atque istius inscia culpae
> descendam magnorum haud umquam indignus avorum.
>
> (12.645–9)

Shall I turn my back, shall this land see Turnus running away? Is it indeed so terrible to die? Shades of the underworld, be kind to me, for the will of the gods above is hostile. I shall come down to you an unsullied soul, free of such a sin as cowardice, never unworthy of my great ancestors.

We hear again, as Turnus says these words, the words of Hector (*Iliad* 22.304 f.): 'Let me not die without a struggle and ingloriously, but having done some great deed for future generations to hear', and more faintly but still unmistakably we hear again the words of Dido in her last moments of life (4.653 f.): 'I have lived, and the course Fortune allotted I have completed, and now my ghost in majesty will pass to the underworld.'

Jupiter decrees that divine assistance for Turnus (from Juno and Juturna) must cease, and he sends down a Fury in the shape of an owl, beating in Turnus' face. Our thoughts go back to the lonely and terrified Dido whose nightmare visions and torments of conscience were accompanied by the long-drawn hooting of an owl (4.462 ff.). There follows the lament of Juturna as the sister says farewell to her brother; there are echoes here of the lamentation of Anna for her sister Dido, as the wildness of grief is described, and both sisters lament their empty future and wish they had died too (12.869 ff., 4.672 ff.). The last scenes of the tragedy of Turnus are thus linked with the tragedy of Dido.

Aeneas challenges Turnus to battle, and magnificent in his hopeless defiance Turnus replies:

> non me tua fervida terrent
> dicta, ferox; di me terrent et Iuppiter hostis.
>
> (12.894–5)

Your hot words do not frighten me, fierce though you be; the gods frighten me, and Jupiter my enemy.

Yet he still fights on; he seizes a huge stone but is like a man in a dream, and cannot hurl it to its mark. Aeneas' spear-cast wounds him, and he begs for mercy as Hector had done (*Iliad* 22.338 ff.). But the opening words of Turnus' plea were not in Hector's speech:

> equidem merui nec deprecor, inquit;
> utere sorte tua.

> (12.931–2)

'I have deserved it,' he said, 'and I do not complain. Use your good fortune.'

This is not a recognition by Turnus that he was in the wrong: it is merely a statement that he has accepted a contest to the death and is prepared to abide by the consequences. It is a last splendid gesture of heroic defiance, and when Aeneas does kill him we feel pity and disquiet.

As with Dido, so with Turnus – Virgil has written partly from the point of view of the defeated. This is the price of Rome – with victory for one side goes defeat for the other. Aeneas' way of life was a better one than Turnus', and intellectually we applaud his victory, but we are not allowed to pretend that there is no more to be said.

Virgil's intention in his poem was to proclaim the message of Rome to mankind, to present her divine mission and extol its benefits; to set it against the sins and sorrows of the world and see whether it would solve them. He exemplifies the theme of suffering in the figure of Juno, hostile to the Roman purpose and therefore planning to bring all possible disaster upon Aeneas and his men. Virgil poses this problem in his invocation to the Muse:

> Musa, mihi causas memora, quo numine laeso
> quidve dolens regina deum tot volvere casus
> insignem pietate virum, tot adire labores
> impulerit. tantaene animis caelestibus irae?

> (1.8–11)

Muse, tell me the reasons – through what insult to her divinity or in anger for what cause did the queen of the gods cause a man outstanding for his devotion to duty to undergo such hardships, to experience such toils? Can there be such great anger in heavenly hearts?

This last phrase summarises the problem of human suffering and the difficulty mortals have in understanding why the good should suffer. Milton translated the phrase in *Paradise Lost* (6.788):

In heavenly spirits could such perverseness dwell?

and stated the purpose of his own poem in a way not dissimilar:

That to the height of this great Argument
I may assert Eternal Providence,
And justify the ways of God to men.

(P.L. 1.24–6)

But Virgil has no positive position of faith like Milton from which he can 'assert Eternal Providence', and unlike Milton he finds only groping and uncertain answers as he explores the problem throughout the poem.

Much of the suffering which comes upon unhappy mortals has already been discussed in connexion with Aeneas in Chapter 3 and with Dido and Turnus in this chapter; it will be enough to give two additional illustrations. The first is the direct work of Juno right at the beginning of the poem; seeing the Trojans almost at their journey's end she persuades Aeolus, god of the winds, to cause a violent storm as a result of which one ship is lost and the rest split into two groups and shipwrecked on the coast of Carthage. This storm symbolises the hostile circumstances which can suddenly and senselessly (as it seems) strike men as they struggle towards a goal which they conceive it to be their duty to reach. Many of the subsequent sufferings which come upon the Trojans are the work of Juno, and in particular her hostility is reiterated at the beginning of the second half of the poem, when she invokes the very powers of the underworld to bring disaster and destruction. Her hostility is finally stopped by Jupiter (12.791 ff.), but not until she has involved her enemies in extreme peril and suffering.

The second illustration is from the end of Book 6. The pageant of Roman heroes waiting to be born has passed before Aeneas' astonished eyes, and his father has summarised for him the nature of Rome's destiny for world civilisation. We expect the book to end here, with the trumpet-notes of triumph for the now inevitable fulfilment of the mission. But it does not. Aeneas asks the identity of a young man shrouded in darkness, and is told of the great grief which his premature death will bring to the Romans. This is Marcellus, son of Octavia, Augustus' sister, who was marked out as Augustus' heir but died at the age of nineteen in 23 BC.

o nate, ingentem luctum ne quaere tuorum;
ostendent terris hunc tantum fata neque ultra
esse sinent. nimium vobis Romana propago
visa potens, superi, propria haec si dona fuissent.

(6.868–71)

My son, do not ask of the deep sorrow of your people. The fates will only give a glimpse of him to earth, and will not let him live beyond that. You gods, the Roman offspring would have seemed too powerful if these gifts had been hers to keep.

Here then is the balance of the *Aeneid*, triumph and disaster, joy and sorrow; it is part of Virgil's special art to have given us a sudden cloud of tragedy when the sky seemed clear.

Does Virgil then find no answer to the question of suffering? No complete answer certainly; yet there are two ways in which his deeply sensitive exploration of these things gropes towards an answer. The first is expressed immediately after the opening description of Juno's hostility:

> tantae molis erat Romanam condere gentem.
>
> (1.33)

So great a task it was to found the Roman race.

The implication of this theme, which runs all through the poem is that greatness is only achieved by great endeavour and so great suffering. It cannot be said that this idea is presented more than tentatively; certainly Aeneas does not feel it to such an extent as to derive certainty and joy from his dedication, and in this way he differs greatly from the early Christian heroes with whom he is often compared. But faint though the concept is it sheds its light in the dark places of the poem.

The second area in which an answer is sought is defined in the sixth book, where Virgil presents a view of the relationship between this life and the after-life which suggests that in some way not fully comprehensible to men virtue is rewarded in a richer life to come. Consider the inhabitants of Virgil's Elysium:

> hic manus ob patriam pugnando vulnera passi,
> quique sacerdotes casti, dum vita manebat,
> quique pii vates et Phoebo digna locuti,
> inventas aut qui vitam excoluere per artis,
> quique sui memores aliquos fecere merendo.
>
> (6.660–4)

Here is the band of those who suffered wounds fighting for their country; those who were pure priests in life, dutiful poets who spoke words worthy of Phoebus, or those who enriched life by discovering new ways of living it, or those who made some remember them by their service.

The last line opens the doors of Elysium to all, however humble, who have deserved to go to heaven.

Virgil expands his ideas (mainly Orphic and Stoic ideas) in the speech of Anchises (6.724 ff.). The world is made of two elements, matter and mind (or spirit); it is the task of everyone to live in such a way as to encourage the spiritual side. Our souls are imprisoned in our bodies as if in a prison, and will be tainted and stained by the things of the body, the more so in proportion to the attention given in life to the things of the body. After death purification takes place and those souls which can be sufficiently purified go to dwell in Elysium and then in the ultimate paradise; the rest drink of the river Lethe to forget their previous lives and are reborn in new bodies.

This is clearly a religion of hope, in very strong contrast with Homeric ideas about the afterlife. For the Homeric hero life on earth was all; it should be lived to the full, for the life after death was thought to be miserable and shadowy. The shade of Achilles told Odysseus (*Odyssey* 11.488 f.): 'I would sooner be the lowest serf on earth than king of all the dead.' The shift to an emphasis on the greater importance of the next life began with the Greek mystery religions, was especially prominent in Orphism and Pythagoreanism, and was assimilated and intellectualised by Plato; many of these Greek views were assimilated in Roman Stoicism. Virgil has presented an amalgam of these ideas, made rather more personal to the individual than was the case in Stoicism, and his poetical presentation has a real impact. Yet this must not be overstressed. The Middle Ages looked upon Virgil as a prophet of Christ, a pre-Christian, partly because of the prophecy of the birth of a child to inaugurate a new Golden Age (*Eclogue* 4) and partly because of the moral and spiritual values of the *Aeneid* which we have been discussing; but Virgil's beliefs were still uncertain, and when at the end of the sixth book Aeneas goes out by the gate of false dreams, we must surely think that Virgil means that the religion of the book is a poetic dream and not a revelation. The point can best perhaps be made by another comparison with Milton: where Milton proclaims the certainty of his doctrine, Virgil gropes towards his ideas in hope, not faith.

The nature of suffering is a cosmic problem to which Virgil's Roman theme had led him. Let us return finally to his Roman theme. In this chapter we have seen how the sensitive poet explored the deepest implications of the Roman world mission and found that there were many problems and uncertainties remaining. But – and this is vitally important – the vision never disappears, it is not eliminated by the passages of pathos. The poem is essentially optimistic in spite of its tears; the bright light of human achievement and human potential to achieve more shines though the dark places. Listen once again to the final phrases of Jupiter's promise:

> aspera tum positis mitescent saecula bellis;
> cana Fides et Vesta, Remo cum fratre Quirinus
> iura dabunt; dirae ferro et compagibus artis
> claudentur Belli portae; Furor impius intus
> saeva sedens super arma et centum vinctus aënis
> post tergum nodis fremet horridus ore cruento.
>
> (1.291–6)

Then wars will be laid aside and the harsh generations become gentle; white-haired Trust and Vesta, goddess of the home, Romulus reconciled with his twin Remus, will administer justice. The gates of War, terrible with their tight iron fastenings, shall be shut: within, wicked Frenzy, sitting on a heap of weapons, his arms bound fast behind his back with a hundred knots of bronze, a ghastly figure with bloodstained lips, shall rage and rage in vain.

The Roman Forum

Index